My Daily Routine in Korean

매일 하는
동작을
한국어로!

written by
TalkToMeInKorean

Introduction

MY DAILY ROUTINE IN KOREAN is a picture dictionary designed to help you learn everyday Korean words and expressions through convenient visual aids. The book is divided into 32 different categories which are related to common everyday activities, and each of the categories introduces up to 17 phrases through fun illustrations. The translation of each phrase is on the reverse page of the illustration, and you can also find an index of all 408 expressions at the end of this book.

With this book, you do not have to memorize every word in order from cover to cover, but if you learn better that way, that's fine, too! The easiest and one of the more productive ways to study with this book is by choosing a topic which interests you and choose one or two words/expressions from that topic to use in your everyday actions and conversations. Read the words or expressions aloud and listen to the MP3 audio pronunciation of the words/expressions if you'd like to hear them spoken by a native speaker, write them down in a notebook, and put them to use! The more you read, write, say, or hear words and expressions in practice, the easier you can recall the word or expression when you need to use it.

MP3 audio files can be downloaded at http://TalkToMeInKorean.com/audio.

CONTENTS

CONTENTS

①

SLEEPING

잠자기

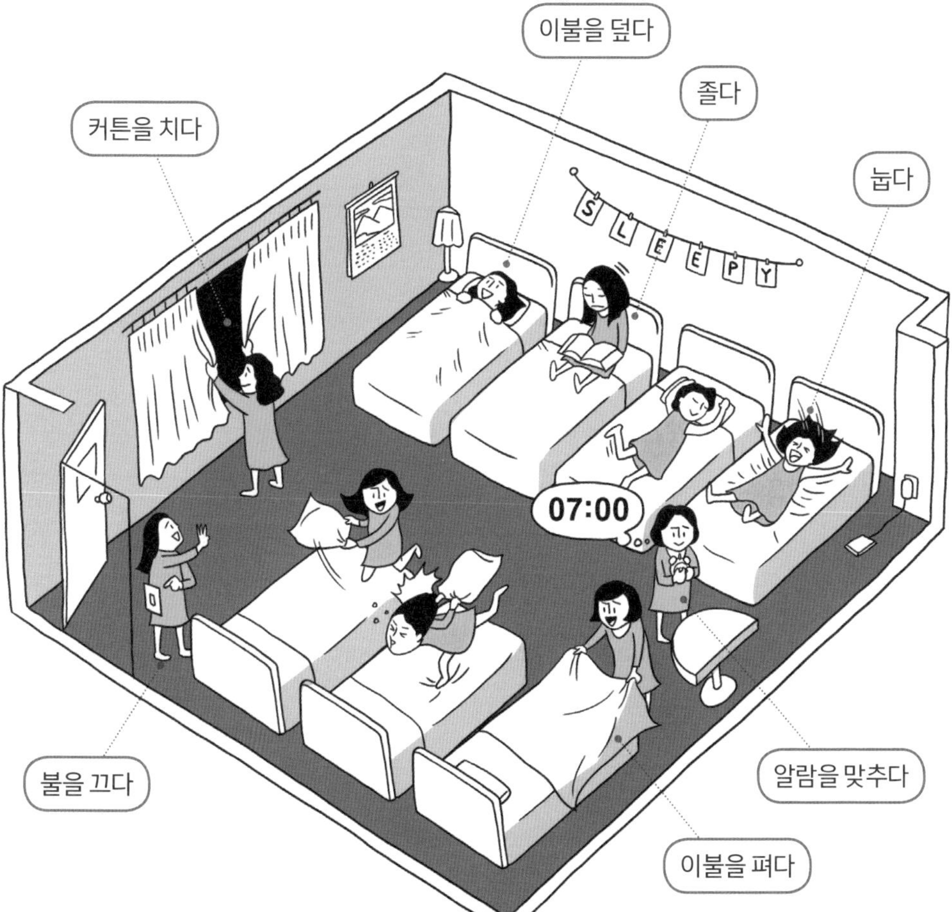

1

잠자기

●○

Track #1

커튼을 치다	to draw/close the curtains
이불을 덮다	to cover oneself with blankets/bedclothes
졸다	to doze off, to nod off
눕다	to lie down
알람을 맞추다	to set the alarm
이불을 펴다	to make the bed; to lay the bedding on the floor
불을 끄다	to turn off the light

1

SLEEPING

잠자기

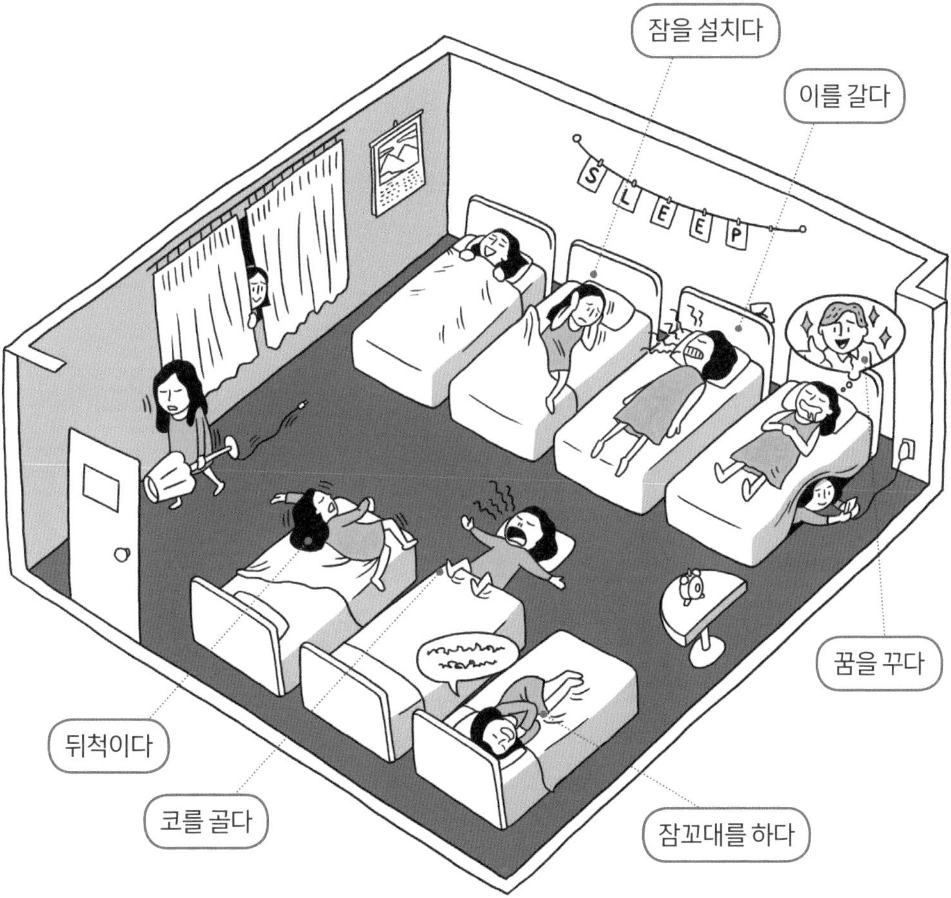

Track #1

잠을 설치다	to have a restless night's sleep, to not sleep well
이를 갈다	to grind one's teeth
꿈을 꾸다	to dream
잠꼬대를 하다	to talk in one's sleep
코를 골다	to snore
뒤척이다	to toss and turn

2

WAKING UP

일어나기

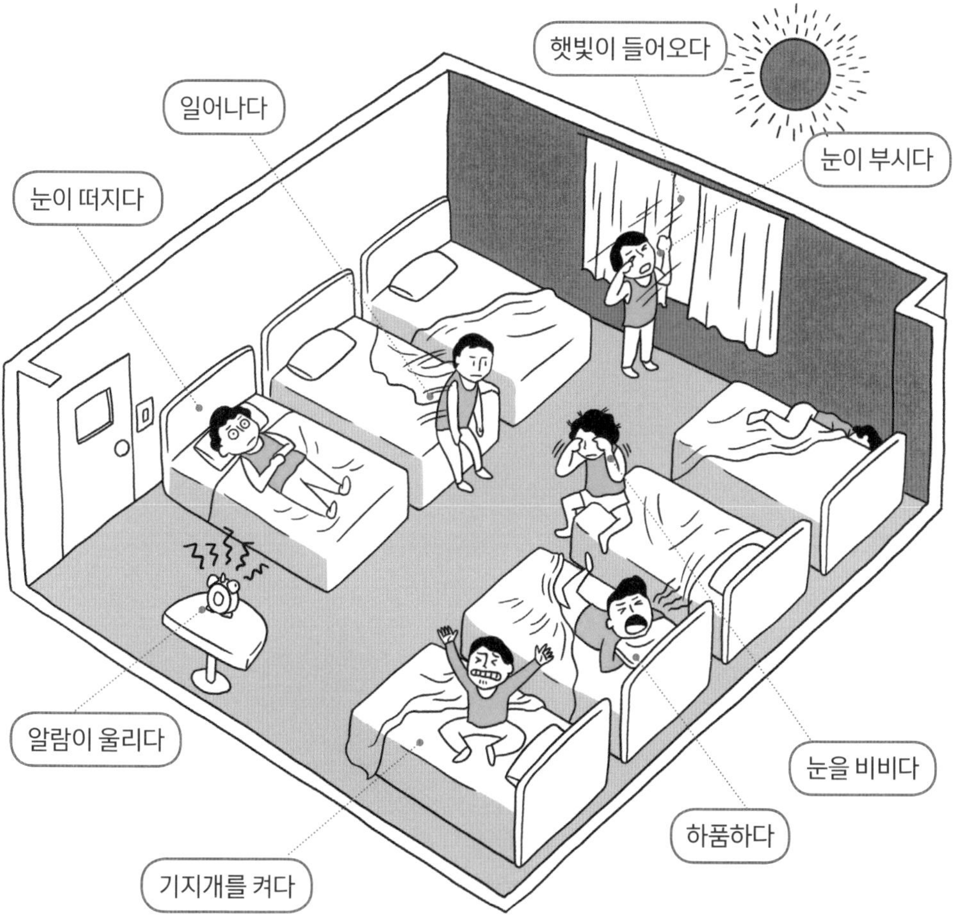

2

일어나기

●○

Track #2

눈이 떠지다	one's eyes open (lit. one's eyes snap open)
일어나다	to get up
햇빛이 들어오다	sunlight shines into [somewhere]
눈이 부시다	to be dazzling; to be very bright
눈을 비비다	to rub one's eyes
하품하다	to yawn
기지개를 켜다	to stretch (after sleep or when one is tired)
알람이 울리다	the alarm goes off

2

WAKING UP

일어나기

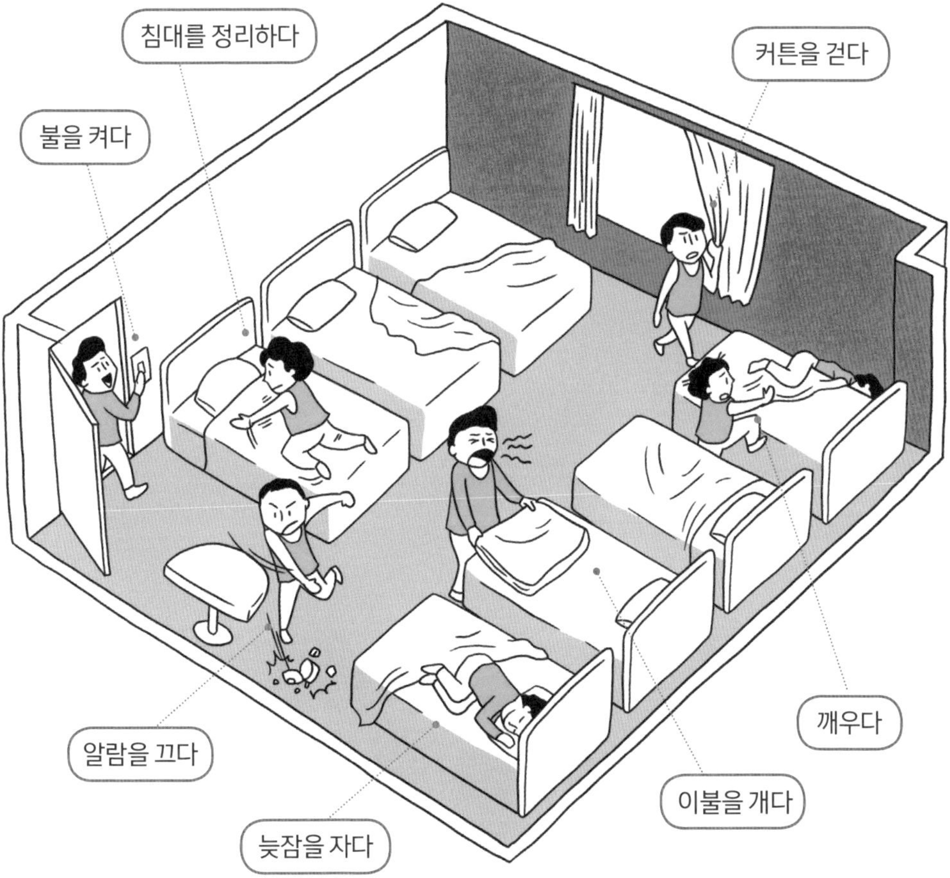

2

일어나기

Track #2

알람을 끄다	to turn off the alarm
불을 켜다	to turn on the lights
침대를 정리하다	to make one's bed
커튼을 걷다	to open the curtains
깨우다	to wake [someone]
이불을 개다	to fold the bedding
늦잠을 자다	to oversleep

3

SHOWERING

샤워하기

3

샤워하기

●○

Track #3

수압이 세다	the water pressure (of the shower) is strong
수압이 약하다	the water pressure (of the shower) is weak
비누칠을 하다	to lather up/put soap on one's body
바디 워시/바디 클렌저를 짜다	to squeeze out body wash/body cleanser
바디 워시/바디 클렌저가 다 떨어지다	body wash/body cleanser runs out
머리를 감다	to wash one's hair
등을 밀다	to wash one's back; to rub one's back with a shower sponge/loofah

3

SHOWERING

샤워하기

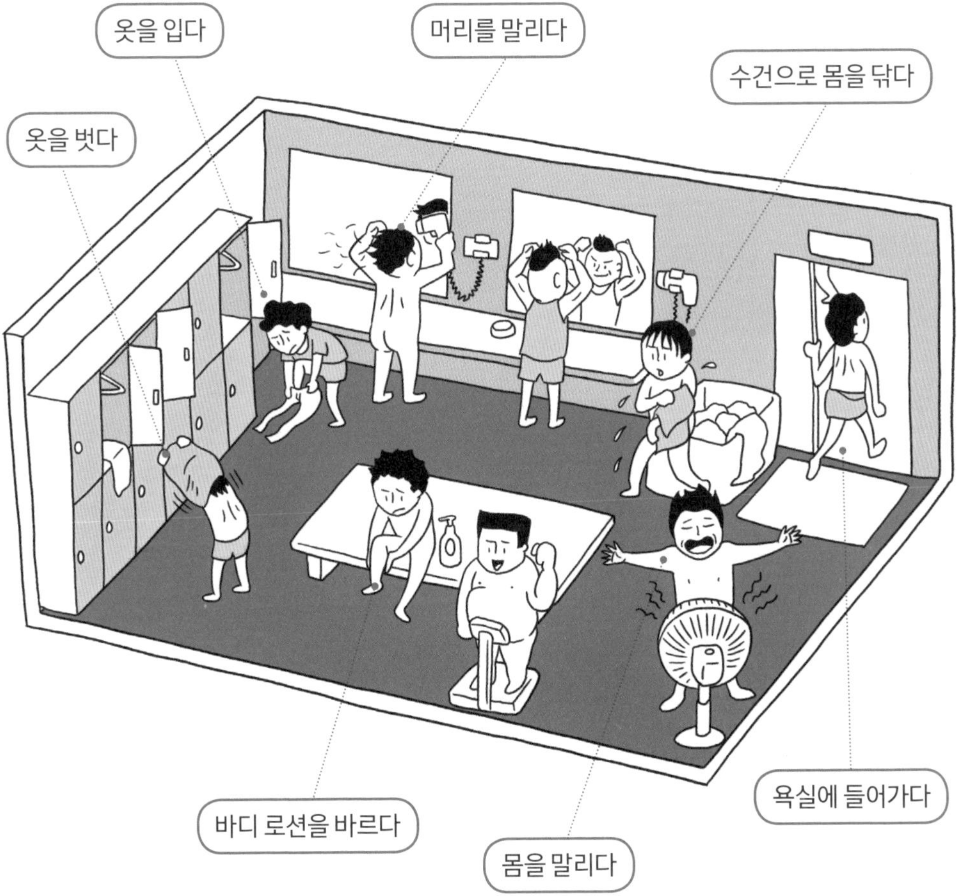

3

샤워하기

Track #3

옷을 벗다	to take off clothes
옷을 입다	to put on clothes
머리를 말리다	to dry one's hair
수건으로 몸을 닦다	to wipe one's body with a towel
욕실에 들어가다	to enter the bathroom
몸을 말리다	to dry one's body
바디 로션을 바르다	to apply body lotion

4

WASHING HAIR

머리 감기

4

머리 감기

●○

Track #4

머리를 감다	to wash one's hair
거품이 나다	to lather
머리를 물로 적시다	to get one's hair wet with water
샴푸가 다 떨어지다	shampoo runs out
샴푸를 짜다	to squeeze out shampoo
머리를 숙이고 감다	to lower one's head and wash one's hair
샴푸를 덜다	to dispense shampoo (lit. to take some shampoo)

4

WASHING HAIR

머리 감기

4

머리 감기

Track #4

두피를 마사지하다	to massage one's scalp
두피를 문지르다	to rub one's scalp
머리를 빗다	to comb one's hair
눈에 샴푸가 들어가다	shampoo gets into one's eyes
머리카락이/머리가 빠지다	hair falls out
머리를 말리다	to dry one's hair

⑤

WASHING FACE

세수하기

Track #5

세수를 하다	to wash one's face
물을 받다	to fill (a basin or bucket) with water
얼굴을 문지르다	to rub one's face
화장솜으로 닦아 내다	to wipe off with a cotton pad
화장을 지우다	to remove one's makeup
세안제를 손바닥에 덜다	to dab/pour some facial cleanser into one's palm
거품을 내다	to lather, to make foam/bubbles

5

WASHING FACE

세수하기

5

세수하기

Track #5

물을 틀다	to turn on the water
거울을 보다	to look in the mirror
눈을 감다	to close one's eyes
얼굴에 물을 묻히다	to put water on one's face
비누를 문지르다	to rub soap (on something)
수건으로 얼굴을 닦다	to wipe one's face with a towel
물로 헹구다	to rinse with water

6

BRUSHING TEETH

양치하기

6

양치하기

●○

Track #6

이를 닦다	to brush one's teeth
입을 벌리다	to open one's mouth
컵에 물을 받다	to fill a cup with water
칫솔을 떨어뜨리다	to drop a toothbrush
남의 칫솔을 쓰다	to use another person's toothbrush
전동 칫솔을 켜다	to turn on an electric toothbrush
가글하다	to gargle
치약을 짜다	to squeeze out toothpaste

6

BRUSHING TEETH

양치하기

6

양치하기

∘•

Track #6

양치하다	to brush one's teeth and gargle
칫솔을 소독하다	to disinfect a toothbrush
칫솔을 말리다	to dry a toothbrush
수건으로 입을 닦다	to wipe off one's mouth with a towel
칫솔을 바꾸다	to change out a toothbrush
입을 헹구다	to rinse one's mouth

7

SHAVING

면도하기

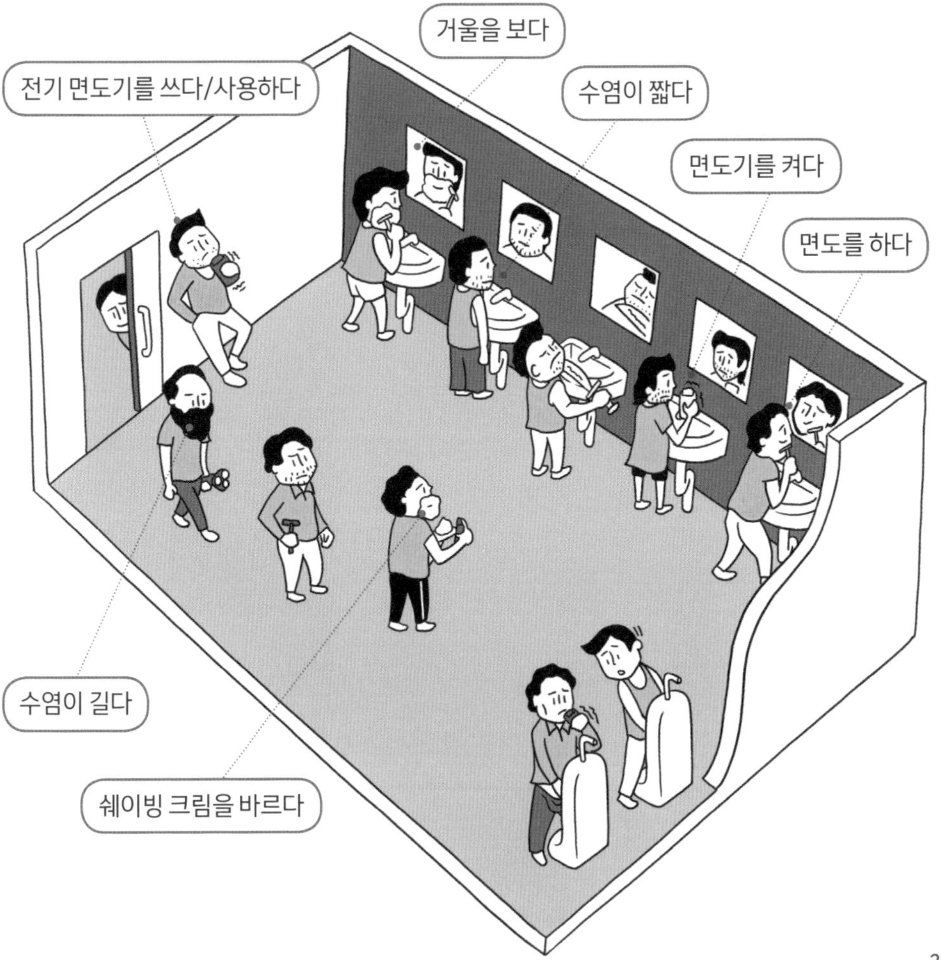

7

면도하기

●○

Track #7

전기 면도기를 쓰다/사용하다	to use an electric shaver
거울을 보다	to look in the mirror
수염이 짧다	to have a short beard/mustache
면도기를 켜다	to turn on an electric shaver
면도를 하다	to shave
쉐이빙 크림을 바르다	to apply shaving cream
수염이 길다	to have a long beard/mustache

7

SHAVING

면도하기

7

면도하기

○●

Track #7

턱을 만지다	to touch one's jaw
깔끔하다	to be neat, to be tidy
씻다	to wash
상처가 나다	to get a nick
면도기를 끄다	to turn off an electric shaver
면도날에 베이다	to get a cut from the blade
수염을 밀다	to shave one's face

8

GLASSES AND CONTACT LENSES

안경과 렌즈

8

안경과 렌즈

●○

Track #8

안경을 쓰다	to wear glasses, to put on one's glasses
안경을 닦다	to clean off one's glasses
안경을 잃어버리다	to lose one's glasses
안경을 찾다	to look for one's glasses, to find one's glasses
안경이 헐겁다	the glasses are too loose
렌즈를 빼다	to take out one's contact lenses
렌즈를 끼다	to wear contact lenses, put in contact lenses

8

GLASSES AND CONTACT LENSES

안경과 렌즈

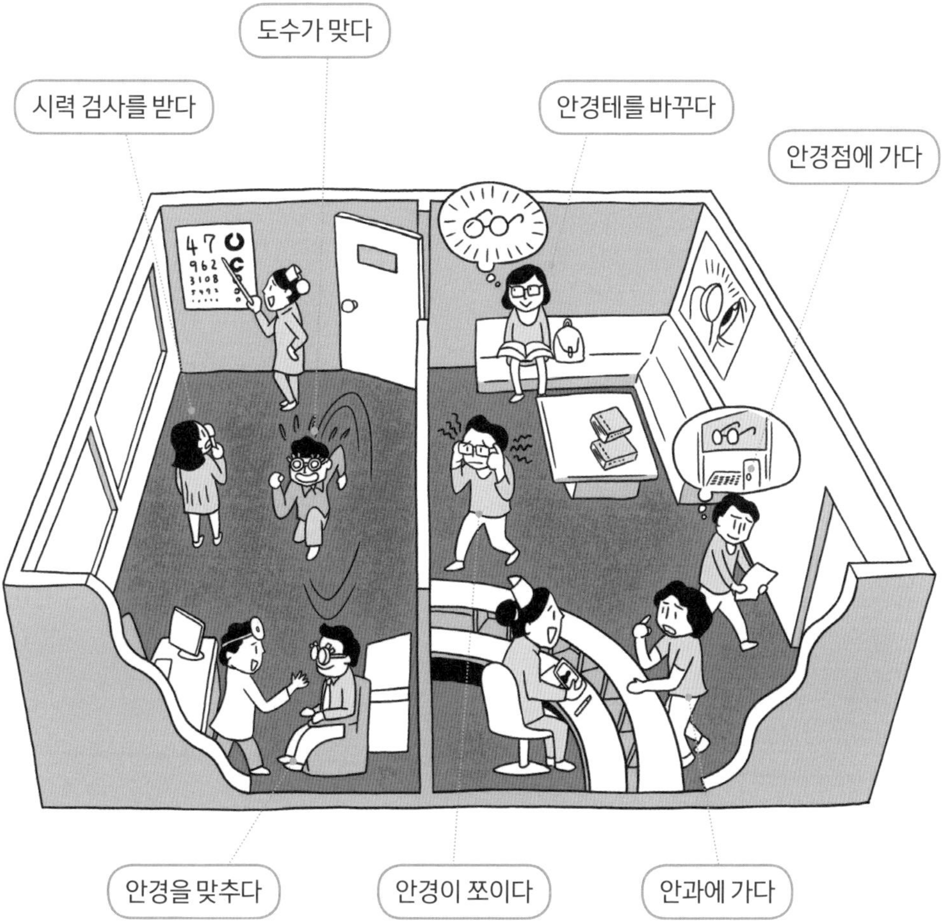

Track #8

시력 검사를 받다	to have one's eyesight checked
도수가 맞다	the prescription for the glasses is correct
안경테를 바꾸다	to change the glasses frame
안경점에 가다	to go to the optician
안과에 가다	to go see an optometrist
안경이 쪼이다	the glasses are too tight
안경을 맞추다	to get a pair of glasses

9

GETTING DRESSED

옷 입기

9

옷 입기

●○

Track #9

옷을 고르다	to pick out clothes
옷에 구멍이 나다	to get a hole in clothing
모자를 쓰다	to put on a hat
옷을 벗다	to take off clothes
옷이 크다	clothes are big
옷이 작다	clothes are small
옷을 입다	to put on clothes
양말을 신다	to put on socks
신발을 신다	to put on shoes

9

GETTING DRESSED

옷 입기

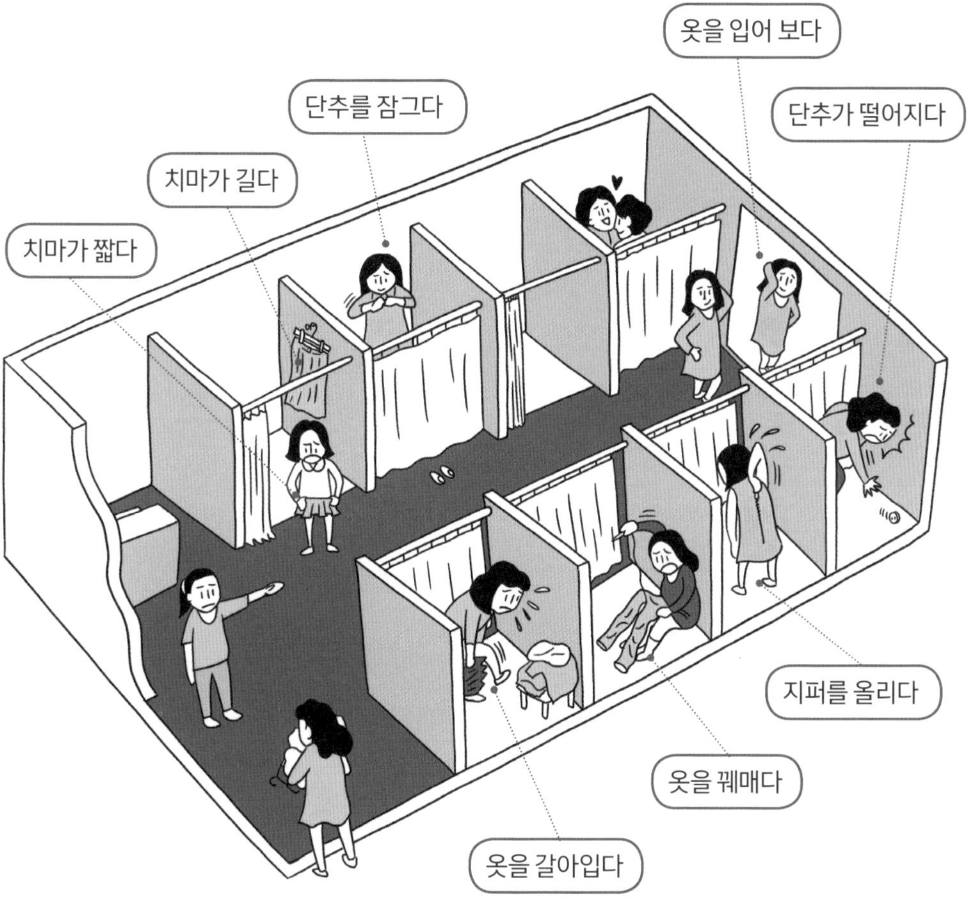

9

옷 입기

∘•

Track #9

치마가 짧다	a skirt is short
치마가 길다	a skirt is long
단추를 잠그다	to button up
옷을 입어 보다	to try on clothes
단추가 떨어지다	a button falls off
지퍼를 올리다	to zip up
옷을 꿰매다	to sew clothes
옷을 갈아입다	to change clothes

10

MAKEUP

화장

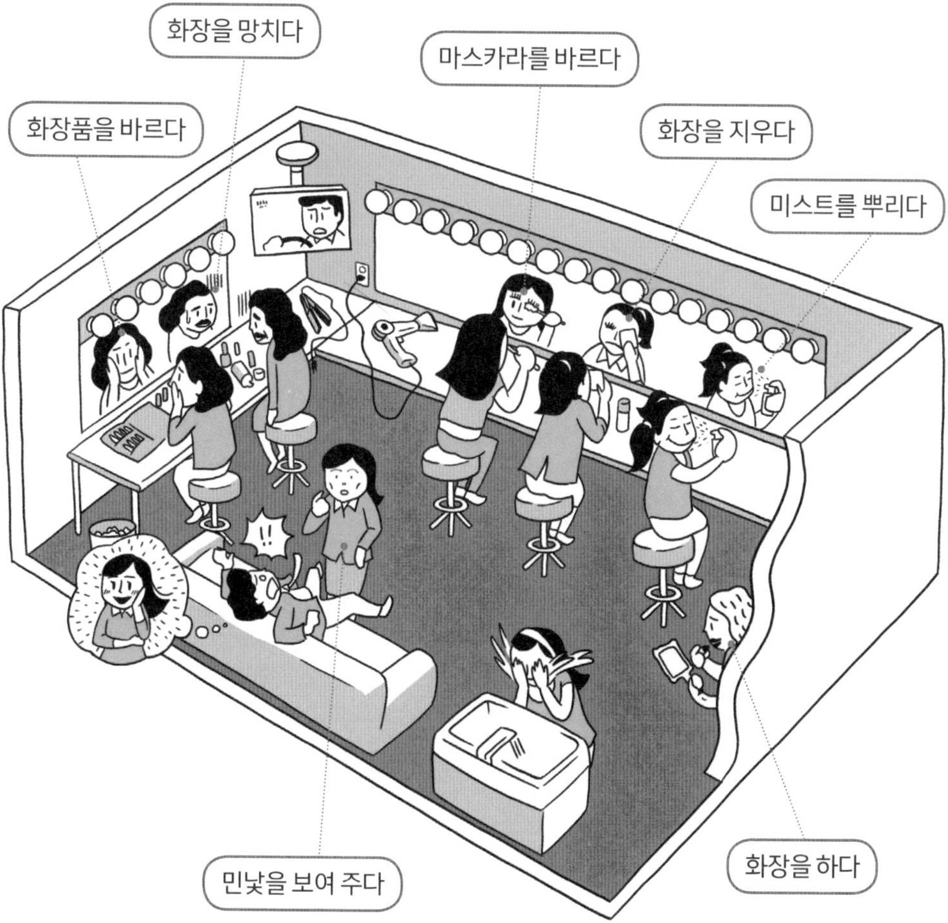

화장을 망치다
마스카라를 바르다
화장품을 바르다
화장을 지우다
미스트를 뿌리다
민낯을 보여 주다
화장을 하다

10

화장

●○

Track #10

화장품을 바르다	to put on makeup products
화장을 망치다	to ruin one's makeup
마스카라를 바르다	to apply mascara
화장을 지우다	to remove one's makeup
미스트를 뿌리다	to spray mist
화장을 하다	to put on makeup
민낯을 보여 주다	to show one's bare face

(10)

MAKEUP

화장

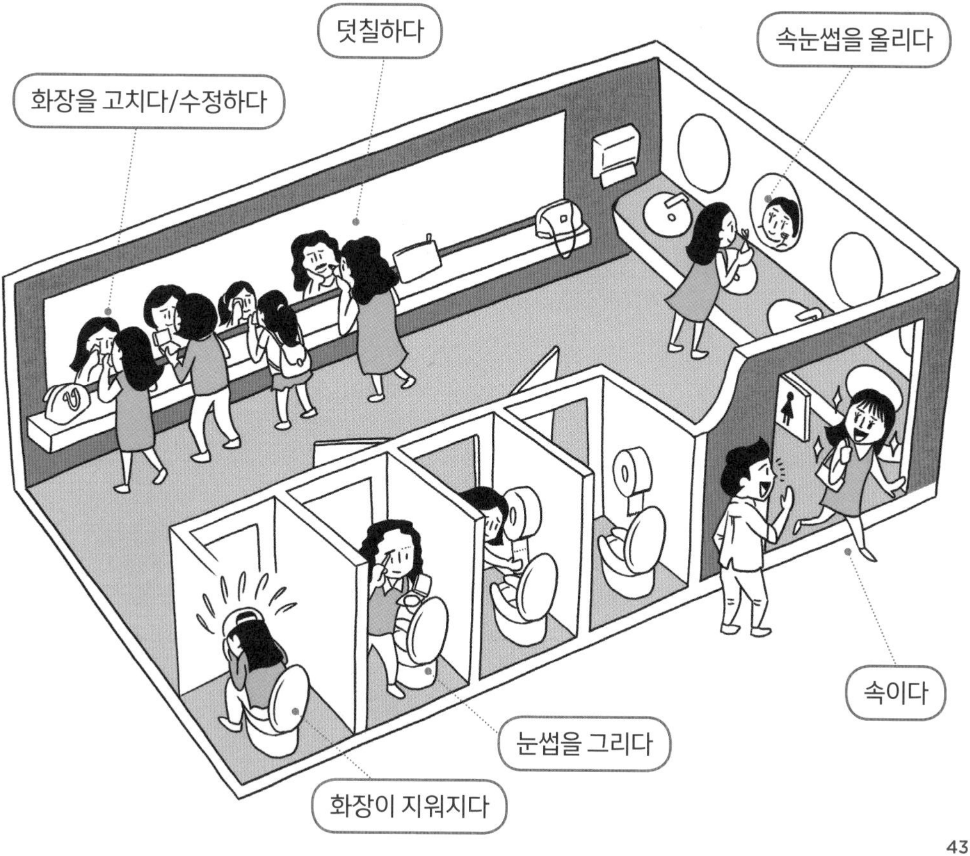
덧칠하다
속눈썹을 올리다
화장을 고치다/수정하다
속이다
눈썹을 그리다
화장이 지워지다

Track #10

화장을 고치다/수정하다	to fix one's makeup
덧칠하다	to paint over
속눈썹을 올리다	to curl the eyelashes (lit. to curl up one's eyelashes)
속이다	to deceive, to trick
눈썹을 그리다	to fill in one's eyebrows (lit. to draw one's eyebrows)
화장이 지워지다	one's makeup is washed away

11

COOKING

요리하기

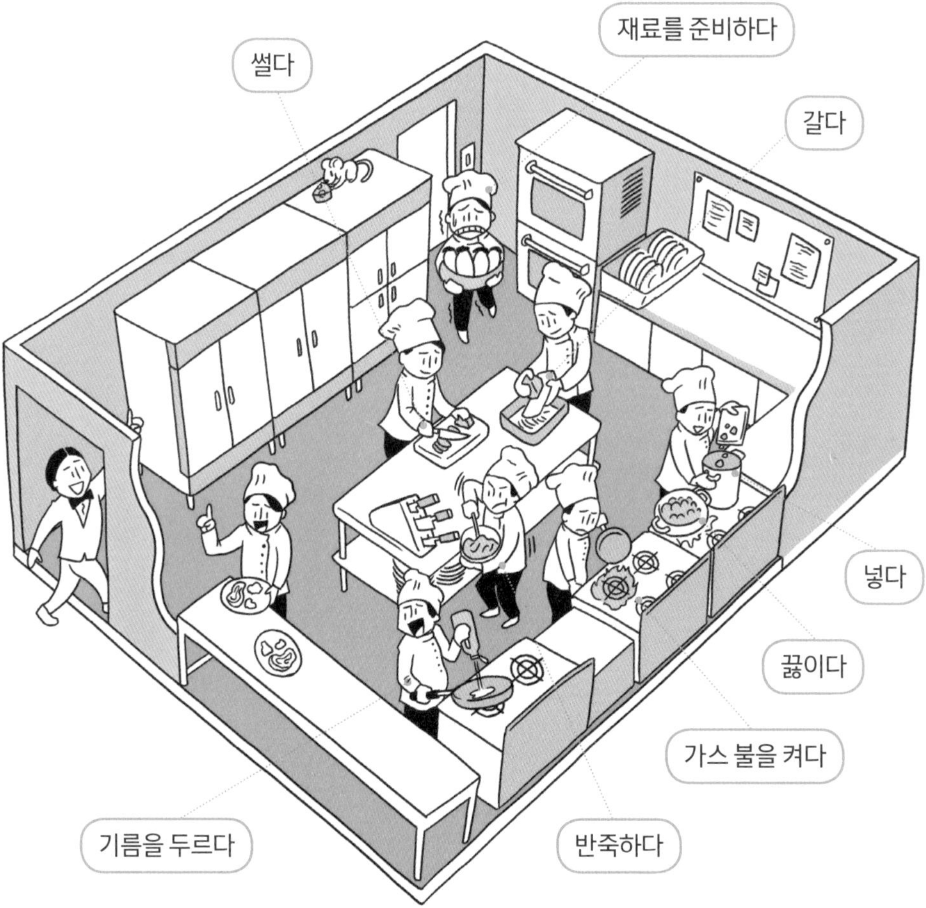

11

요리하기

●○

Track #11

썰다	to cut; to chop
재료를 준비하다	to prepare the ingredients
갈다	to grind
넣다	to add
끓이다	to boil
가스 불을 켜다	to turn on the gas stove
반죽하다	to knead
기름을 두르다	to oil the frying pan

11

COOKING

요리하기

11

요리하기

○●

Track #11

냄비를 태우다	to burn the pot
굽다	to bake
오븐에 넣다	to put into the oven
시간을 재다	to measure the time, to keep time
간을 보다	to taste [something]
태우다	to burn
볶다	to stir-fry

12

EATING

음식 먹기

Track #12

밥을 흘리다	to spill food
반찬 투정을 하다	to complain about side dishes
젓가락으로 집다	to pick [something] up with chopsticks
씹다	to chew
숟가락으로 뜨다	to scoop [something] with a spoon
마시다	to drink
반찬을 놓다	to set the side dishes

12

EATING

음식 먹기

Track #12

밥을 남기다	to not finish a meal, to not eat all of one's food
베어 먹다	to bite, to take a bite
삼키다	to swallow
숟가락, 젓가락을 식탁에 놓다	to put spoons and chopsticks on the table
밥을 푸다	to scoop cooked rice

13

DOING THE DISHES

설거지하기

Track #13

고무장갑을 끼다	to put on rubber gloves
앞치마를 입다	to put on an apron
세제를 덜다	to dispense detergent (lit. to take some detergent [from the container])
식기 세척기에 그릇을 넣다	to put dishes in the dishwasher
그릇이 서로 부딪치다	dishes bump against each other
수세미에 세제를 짜다	to squeeze detergent onto a dish sponge
그릇을 물에 담그다	to put dishes in water
그릇을 닦다	to wipe dishes; to polish dishes

13

DOING THE DISHES

설거지하기

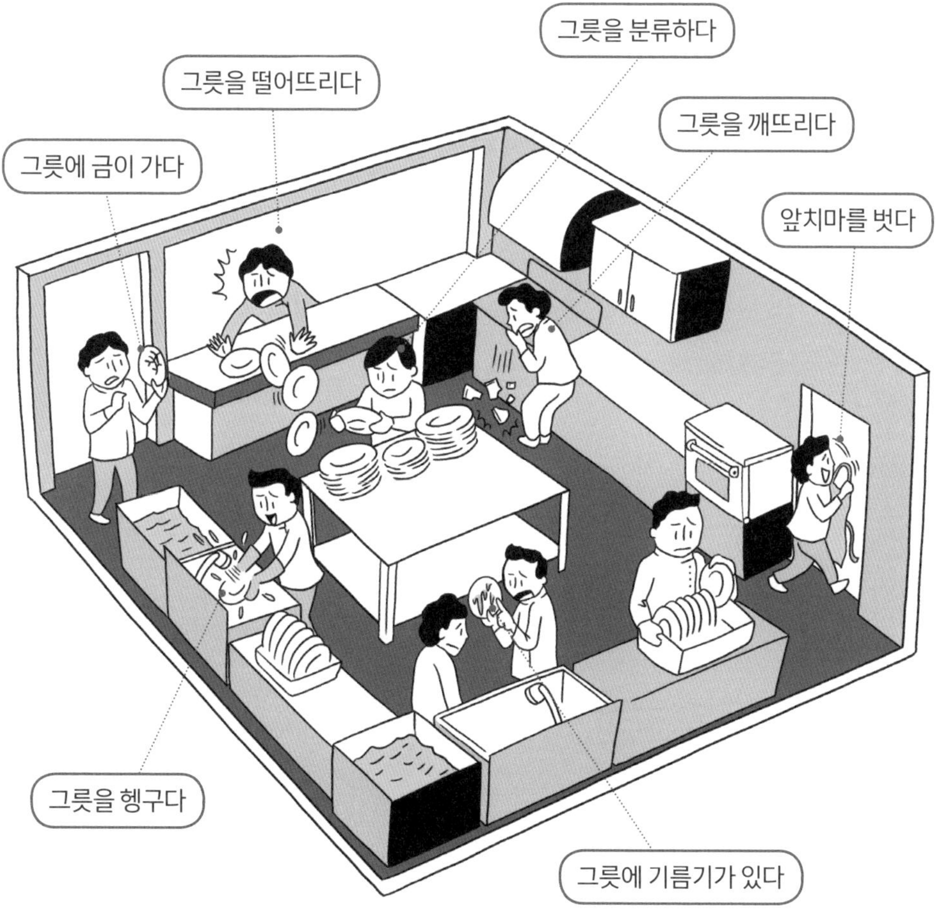

13

설거지하기

Track #13

그릇에 금이 가다	a dish gets cracked
그릇을 떨어뜨리다	to drop a dish
그릇을 분류하다	to sort dishes
그릇을 깨뜨리다	to break a dish
앞치마를 벗다	to take off an apron
그릇에 기름기가 있다	a dish is oily
그릇을 헹구다	to rinse a dish

14

CLEANING

청소하기

●○

14

청소하기

●○

Track #14

물건을 꺼내다	to take items out of a container or drawer
가구를 들다	to lift furniture
청소기를 돌리다	to use the vacuum cleaner
유리창을 닦다	to wipe the glass window, to clean the glass window
먼지를 털다	to dust
바닥을 쓸다	to sweep the floor
플러그를 꽂다	to plug in

14

CLEANING

청소하기

Track #14

플러그를 뽑다	to unplug
가구를 옮기다	to move furniture
창문을 열다	to open the window
환기시키다	to ventilate
바닥을 닦다	to wipe the floor
물건을 제자리에 놓다	to put items back where they belong
청소기 필터를 갈다	to change the filter in the vacuum cleaner

15

LAUNDRY

빨래

15

빨래

●○

Track #15

세탁기를 돌리다	to use the washing machine
빨래를 세탁기에서 빼다	to take laundry out of the washing machine
세제를 넣다	to put in detergent
빨랫감을 분류하다	to sort/separate laundry
건조하다	to dry
얼룩을 지우다	to remove a stain
빨래를 세탁기에 넣다	to put laundry in the washing machine

15

LAUNDRY

빨래

15

빨래

○●

Track #15

세탁소에 옷을 맡기다	to take one's clothes to the cleaner's
세탁소에서 옷을 찾다	to retrieve one's clothes from the cleaner's
빨래를 개다	to fold the laundry
빨래를 널다	to hang the wash out (to dry)
손으로 빨다	to handwash
헹구다	to rinse

16

GARDENING

정원 가꾸기

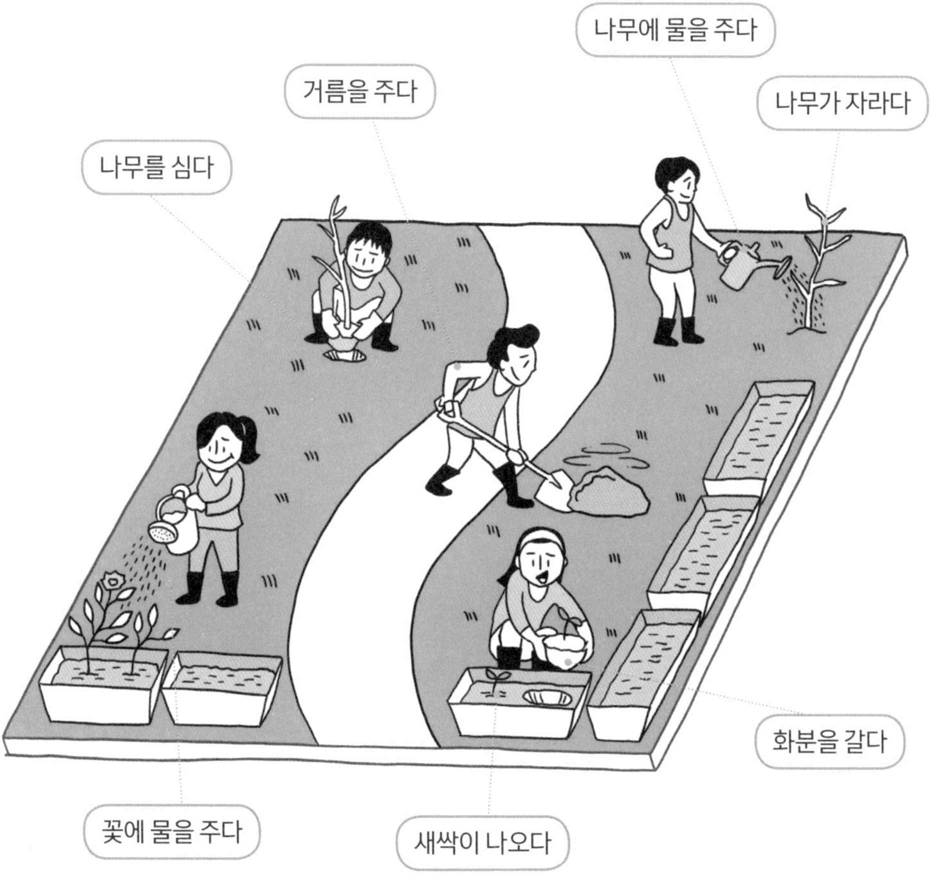

16

정원 가꾸기

●○

Track #16

나무를 심다	to plant a tree
거름을 주다	to apply fertilizer
나무에 물을 주다	to water a tree
나무가 자라다	a tree grows
화분을 갈다	to change pots
새싹이 나오다	to sprout (lit. a shoot/bud comes out [of the ground])
꽃에 물을 주다	to water a flower

16

GARDENING

정원 가꾸기

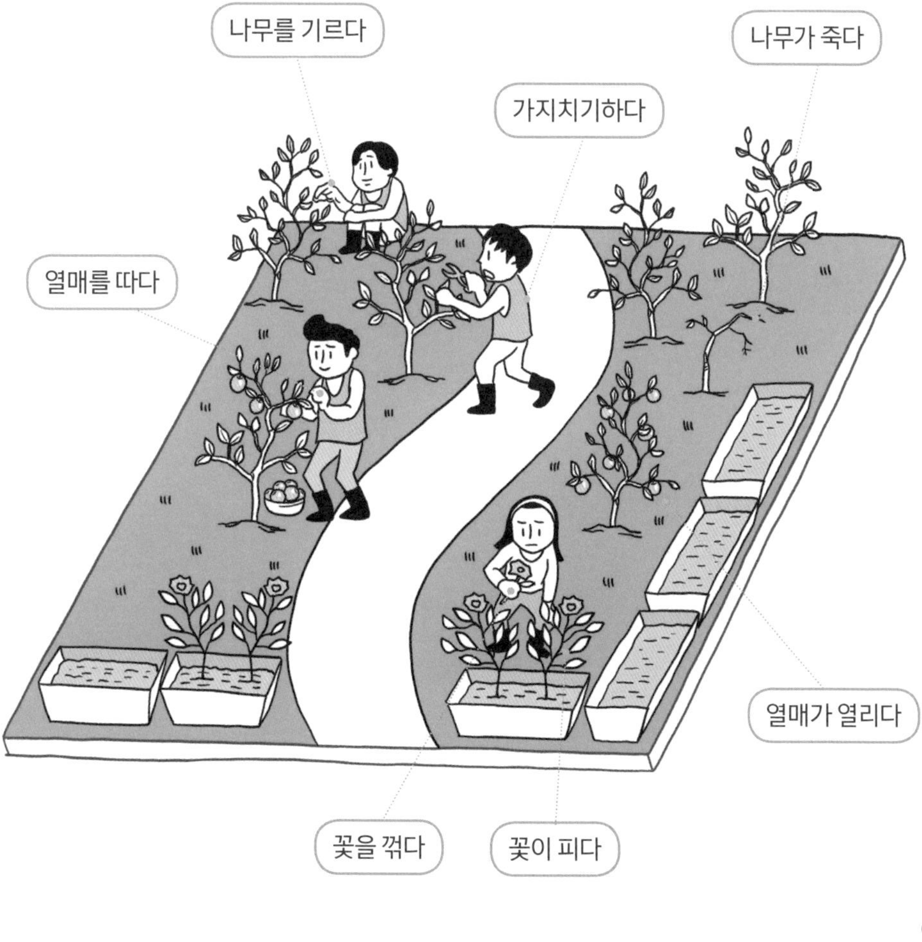

16

정원 가꾸기!

Track #16

나무를 기르다	to grow a tree
가지치기하다	to prune
나무가 죽다	a tree dies
열매가 열리다	to bear fruits
꽃이 피다	a flower blooms
꽃을 꺾다	to pick a flower
열매를 따다	to pick a fruit

17

TELEPHONE

전화

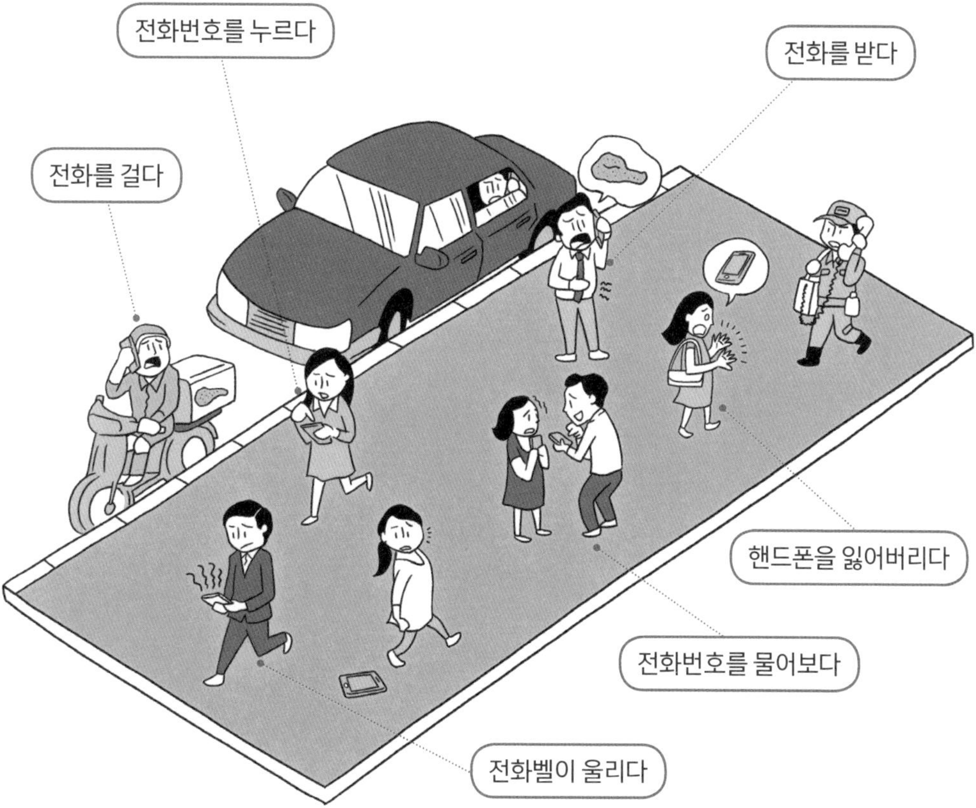

17

전화

●○

Track #17

전화를 걸다	to dial, to make a phone call
전화번호를 누르다	to press the number buttons on a phone
전화를 받다	to receive a phone call
핸드폰을 잃어버리다	to lose a mobile phone
전화번호를 물어보다	to ask for one's phone number
전화벨이 울리다	a phone rings

(17)

TELEPHONE

전화

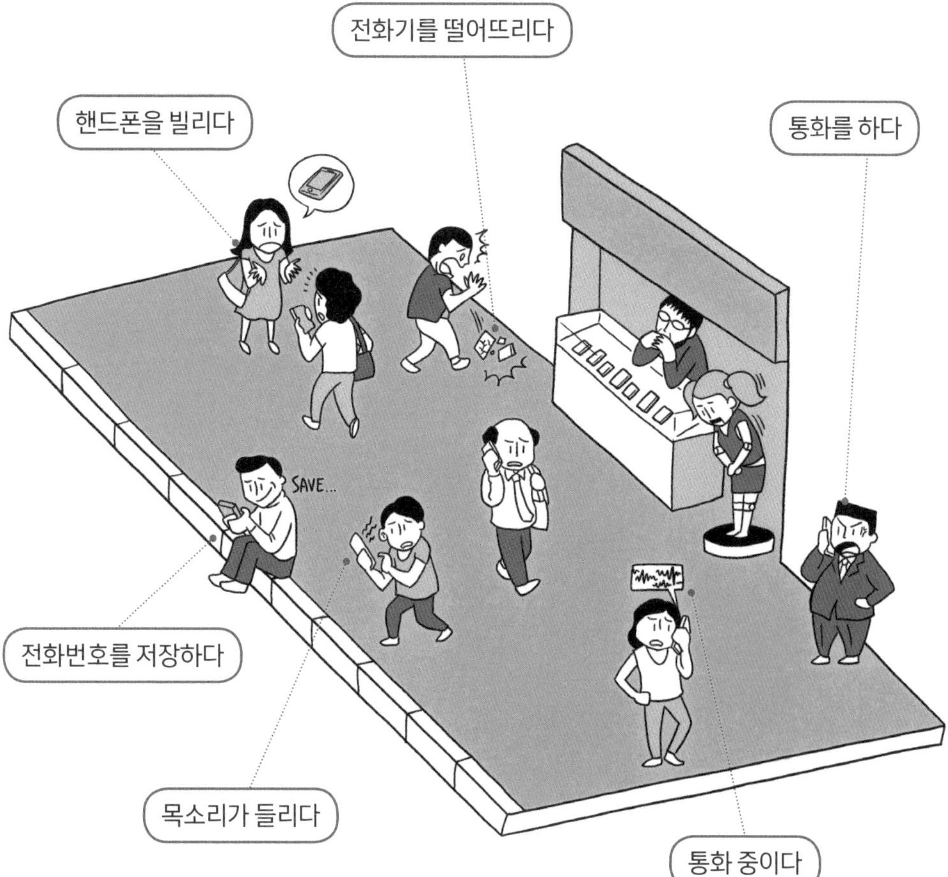

17

전화

○●

Track #17

핸드폰을 빌리다	to borrow a mobile phone
전화기를 떨어뜨리다	to drop a phone
통화를 하다	to talk over the phone
통화 중이다	to be on the phone; the line is busy
목소리가 들리다	a voice is heard; can hear one's voice
전화번호를 저장하다	to save one's phone number

18

TELEVISION

텔레비전

●○

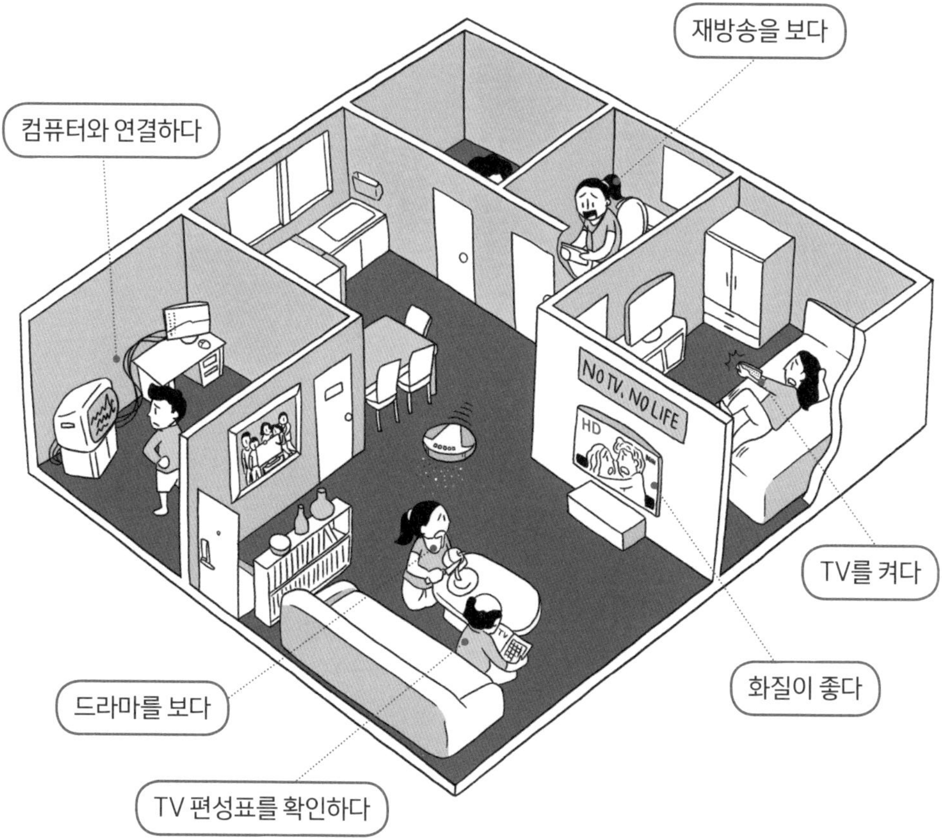

Track #18

컴퓨터와 연결하다	to connect to a computer
재방송을 보다	to watch a rerun
TV를 켜다	to turn on the TV
화질이 좋다	to have a clear picture
TV 편성표를 확인하다	to check the TV guide
드라마를 보다	to watch a TV drama

18

TELEVISION

텔레비전

18

텔레비전

○●

Track #18

화면이 나오다	the TV screen works
TV에 출연하다	to appear on TV, to be on TV
TV를 끄다	to turn off the TV
채널을 돌리다	to switch channels
케이블 TV를 설치하다	to install cable TV
TV를 보다	to watch TV

*TV is pronounced as 티비, and it is also called 텔레비전.

19
RADIO
라디오

신호가 잘 안 잡히다
소리를 키우다
라디오에 사연을 보내다
음악을 틀다
신청곡을 보내다
라디오를 듣다
라디오를 켜다

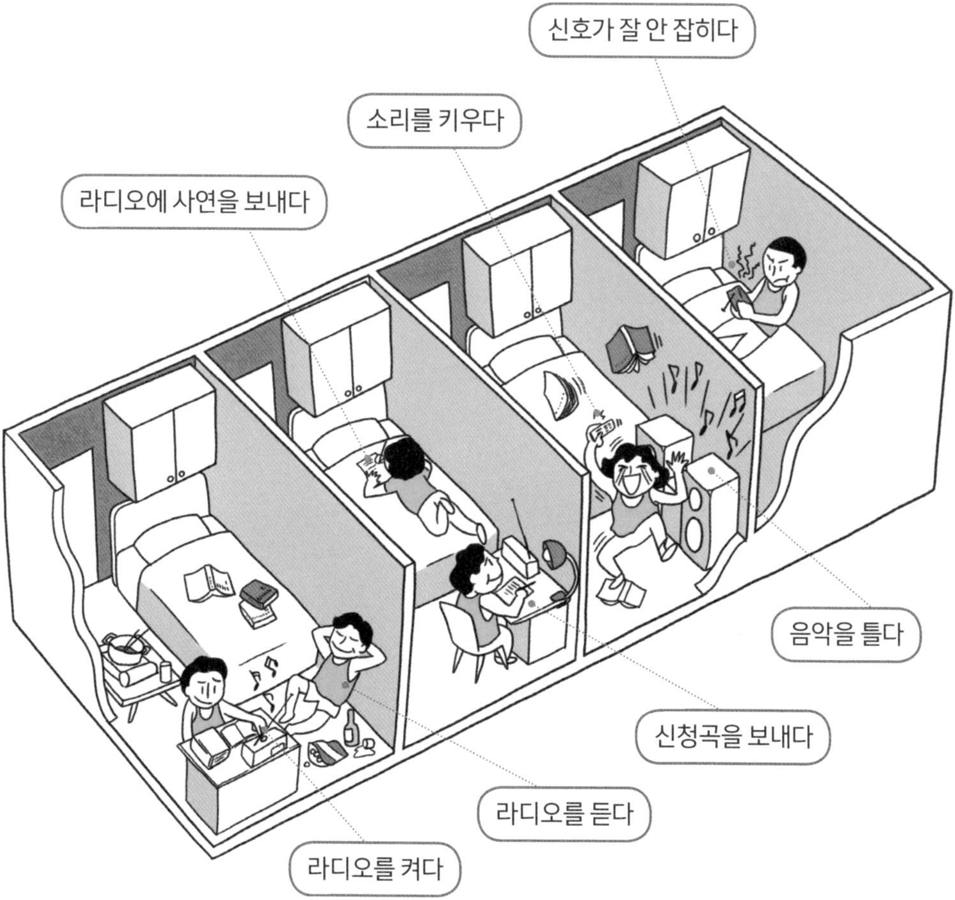

19

라디오

●○

Track #19

라디오에 사연을 보내다	to send a message to a radio show
소리를 키우다	to turn up the volume
신호가 잘 안 잡히다	the signal is bad
음악을 틀다	to play music
신청곡을 보내다	to send in a song request
라디오를 듣다	to listen to the radio
라디오를 켜다	to turn on the radio

19

RADIO

라디오

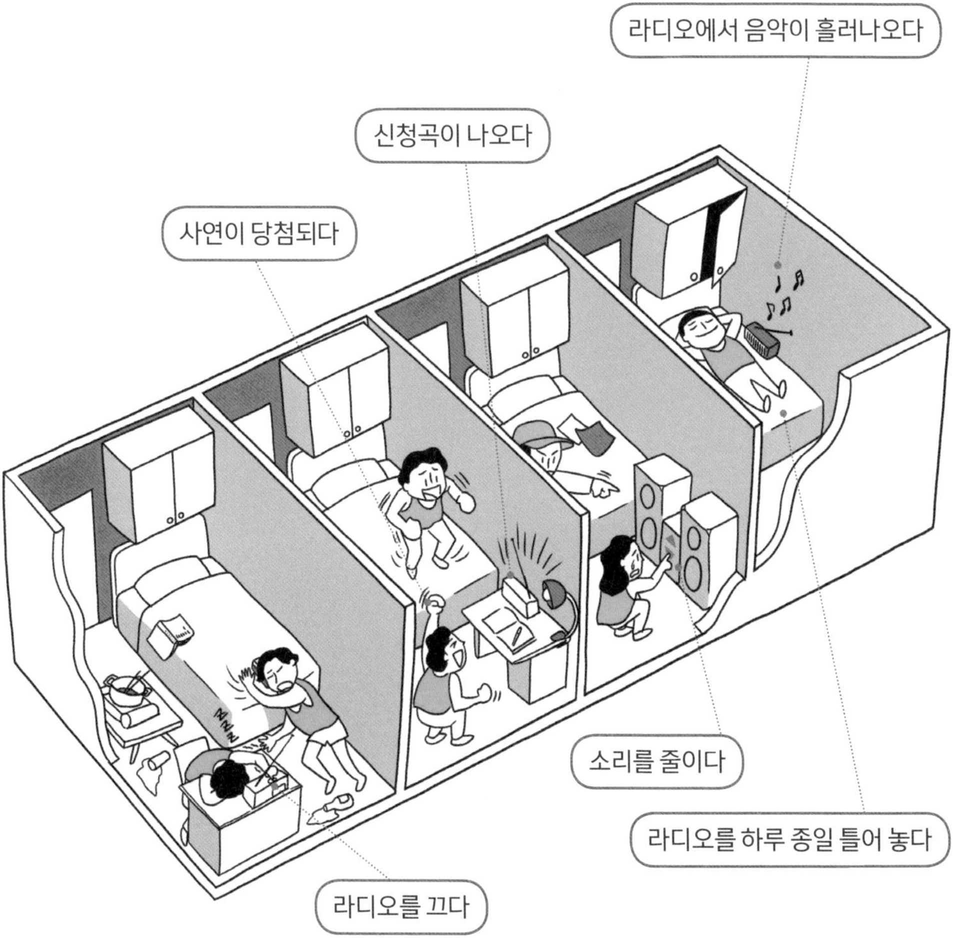
라디오에서 음악이 흘러나오다
신청곡이 나오다
사연이 당첨되다
소리를 줄이다
라디오를 하루 종일 틀어 놓다
라디오를 끄다

19

라디오

∘•

Track #19

사연이 당첨되다	to have one's message picked by (a radio show)
신청곡이 나오다	to hear one's requested song
라디오에서 음악이 흘러나오다	music is played on the radio
라디오를 하루 종일 틀어 놓다	to have the radio on all day long
소리를 줄이다	to turn down the volume
라디오를 끄다	to turn off the radio

20

WEB SURFING

웹서핑

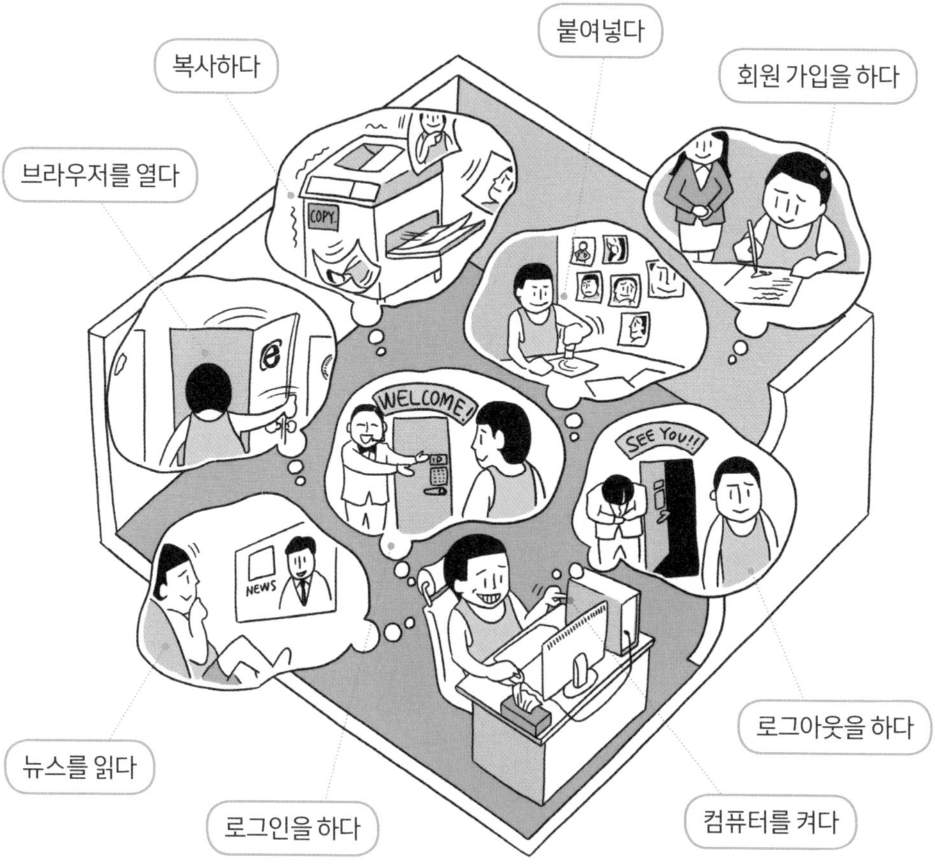

20

웹서핑

●○

Track #20

브라우저를 열다	to open the web browser
복사하다	to copy
붙여넣다	to paste
회원 가입을 하다	to sign up
로그아웃을 하다	to log out
컴퓨터를 켜다	to turn on the computer
로그인을 하다	to log in
뉴스를 읽다	to read the news

20

WEB SURFING

웹서핑

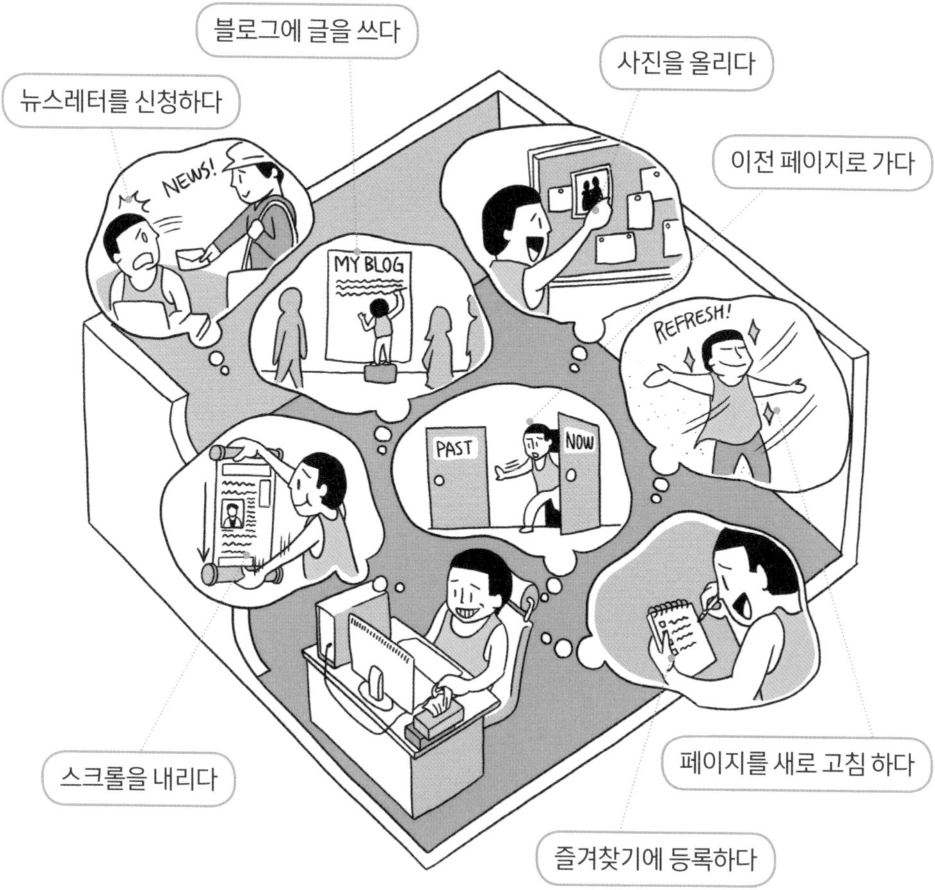

20

웹서핑

○●

Track #20

뉴스레터를 신청하다	to subscribe to a newsletter
블로그에 글을 쓰다	to write in one's blog
사진을 올리다	to post a photo
이전 페이지로 가다	to go to the previous page
페이지를 새로 고침 하다	to refresh the page
즐겨찾기에 등록하다	to add to bookmarks
스크롤을 내리다	to scroll down

21

READING A BOOK

책 읽기

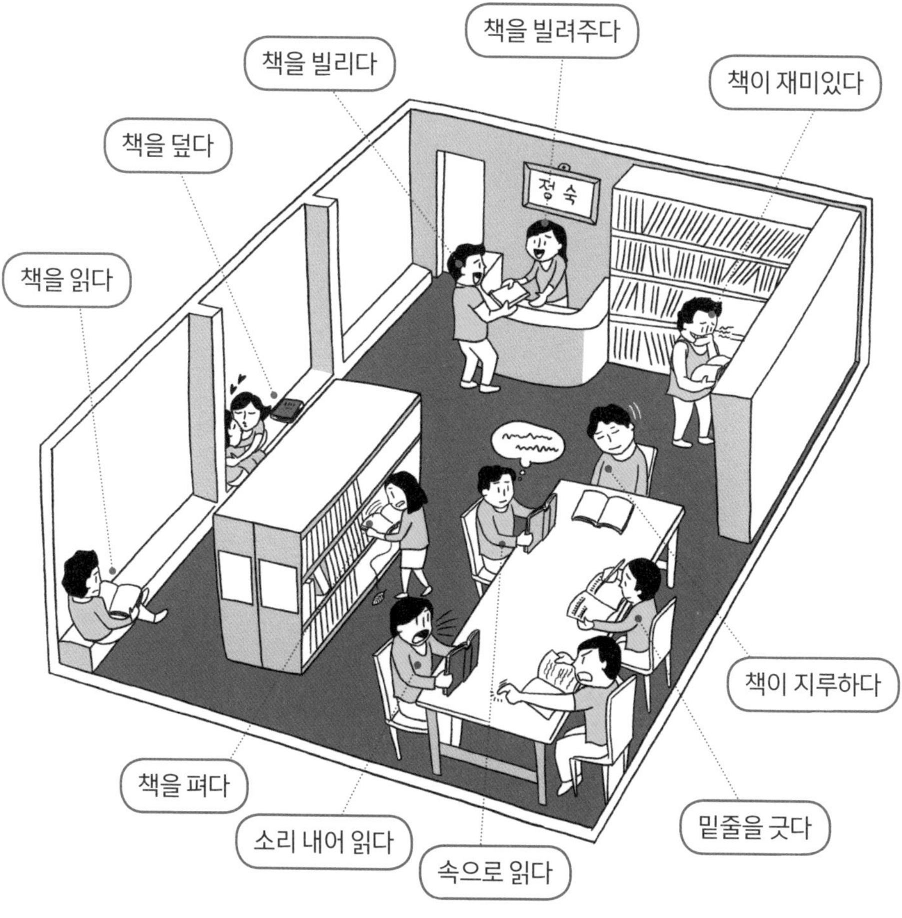

21
책 읽기

Track #21

책을 읽다	to read a book
책을 덮다	to close a book
책을 빌리다	to borrow a book
책을 빌려주다	to lend a book
책이 재미있다	the book is interesting
책이 지루하다	the book is boring
밑줄을 긋다	to underline
속으로 읽다	to read silently, to read to oneself
소리 내어 읽다	to read aloud
책을 펴다	to open a book

22

SITTING

앉기

●○

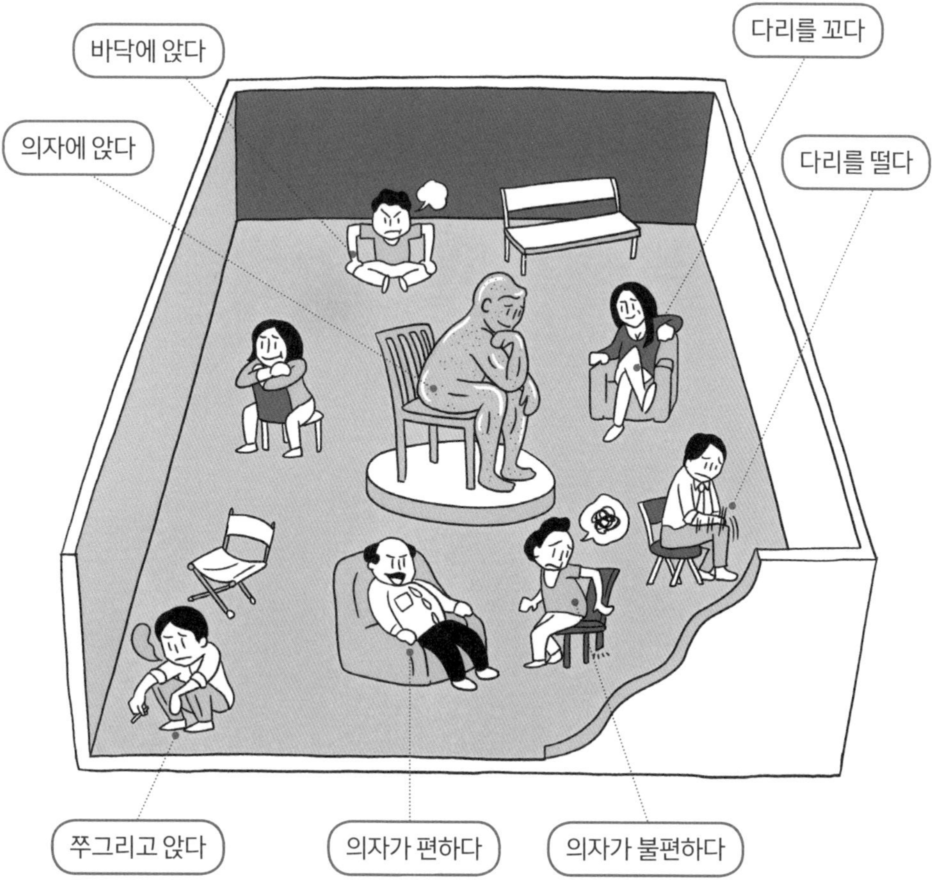

22

앉기

●○

Track #22

의자에 앉다	to sit on a chair
바닥에 앉다	to sit on the floor
다리를 꼬다	to cross one's legs
다리를 떨다	to shake one's leg
의자가 불편하다	a chair is uncomfortable
의자가 편하다	a chair is comfortable
쭈그리고 앉다	to crouch

22

SITTING

앉기

22

앉기

○●

Track #22

의자를 뒤로 젖히다	to recline the seatback of a chair
의자를 바로 세우다	to put up the seatback of a chair
자리가 좁다	to have a small space (to sit)
등받이에 기대다	to lean against the backrest
방석을 깔고 앉다	to sit on a cushion
끼어 앉다	to sit between (two people)

23

LYING DOWN

눕기

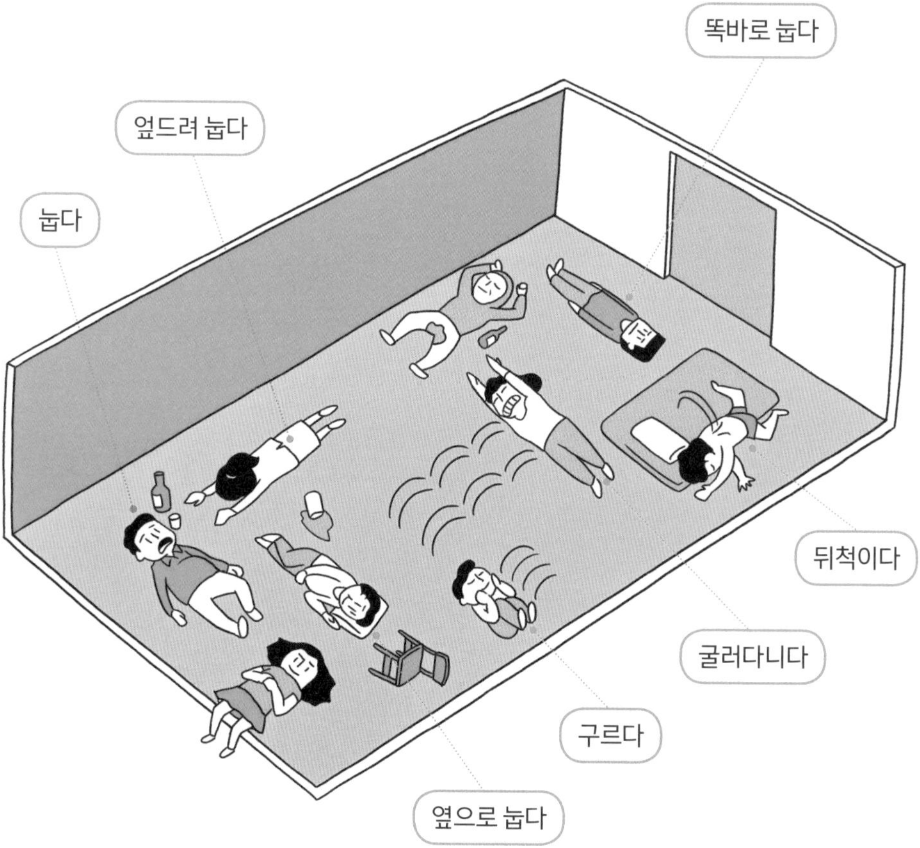

23

눕기

●○

Track #23

눕다	to lie down
엎드려 눕다	to lie on one's face
똑바로 눕다	to lie on one's back
뒤척이다	to toss and turn
굴러다니다	to roll around
구르다	to roll
옆으로 눕다	to lie on one's side

23

LYING DOWN

눕기

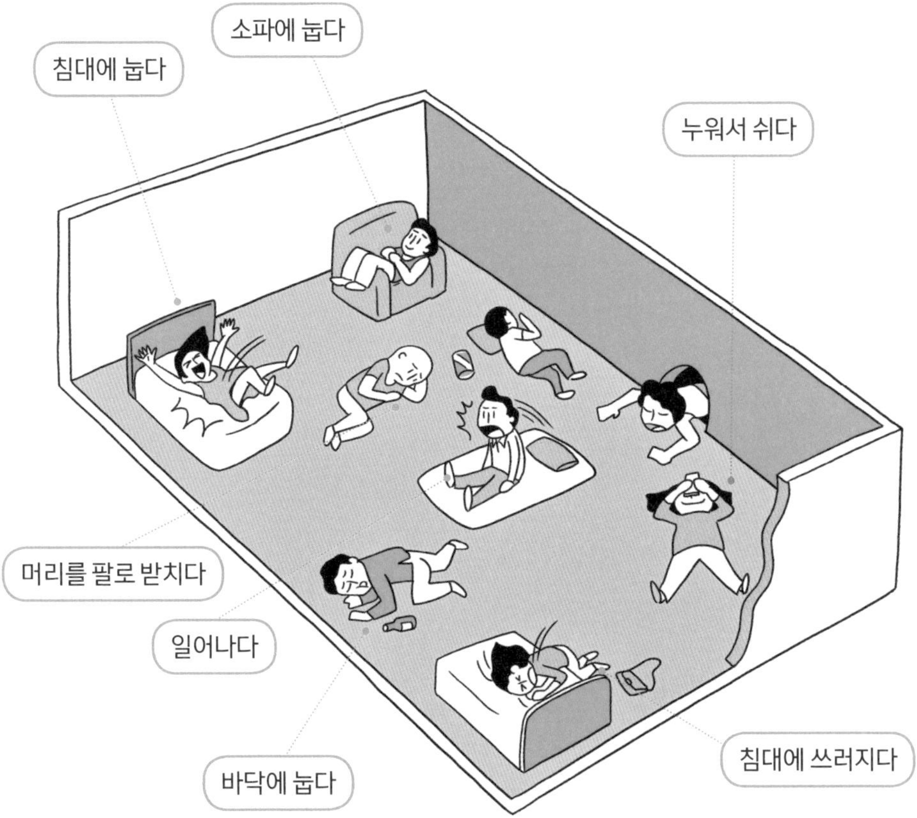

23

눕기

○●

Track #23

침대에 눕다	to lie on a bed
소파에 눕다	to lie on a couch
누워서 쉬다	to lie down and rest
침대에 쓰러지다	to fall onto one's bed
바닥에 눕다	to lie on the floor
일어나다	to get up
머리를 팔로 받치다	to support one's head with an arm

24

STANDING

서기

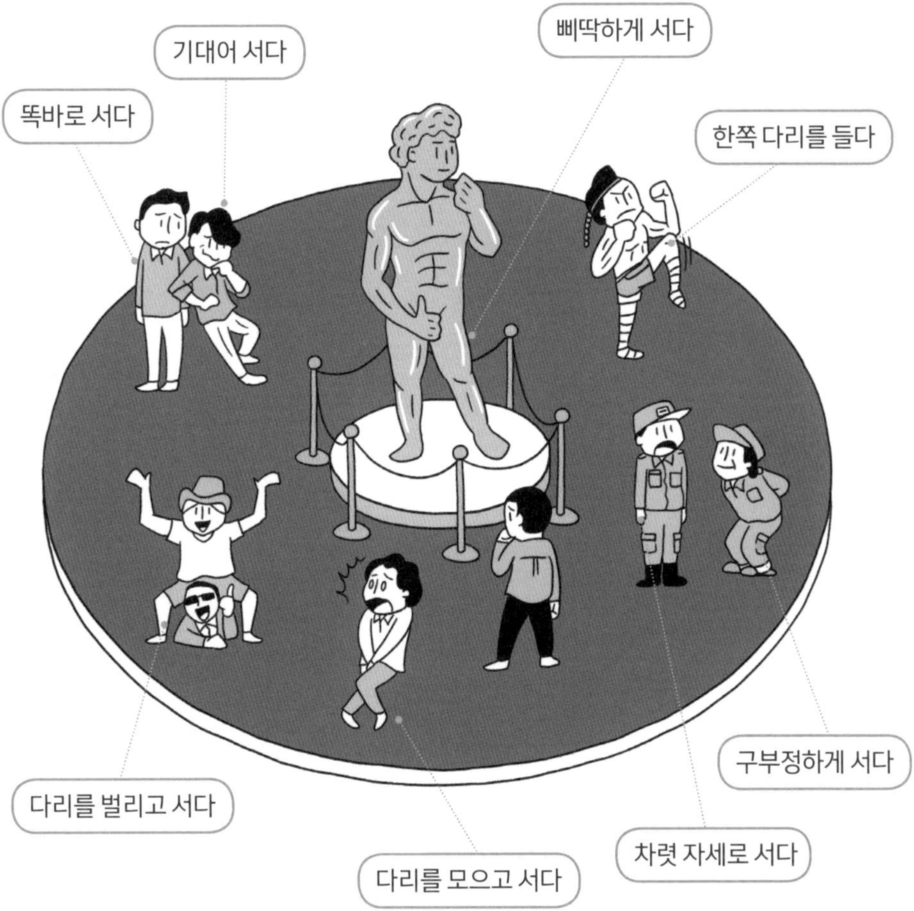

24

서기

●○

Track #24

똑바로 서다	to stand up straight
기대어 서다	to stand leaning against [something]
삐딱하게 서다	to stand with one's head tilted; to not stand straight
한쪽 다리를 들다	to raise one's leg
구부정하게 서다	to slouch while standing
차렷 자세로 서다	to stand at attention
다리를 모으고 서다	to stand with legs together
다리를 벌리고 서다	to stand with legs apart

(24)

STANDING

서기

○●

24

서기

○●

Track #24

서서 관람하다	to stand (while) watching
손을 주머니에 넣고 서 있다	to stand keeping one's hands in one's pocket
서서 일하다	to stand (while) working
줄을 서다	to stand in line
서서 기다리다	to stand (while) waiting

25

HEARING

듣기

●○

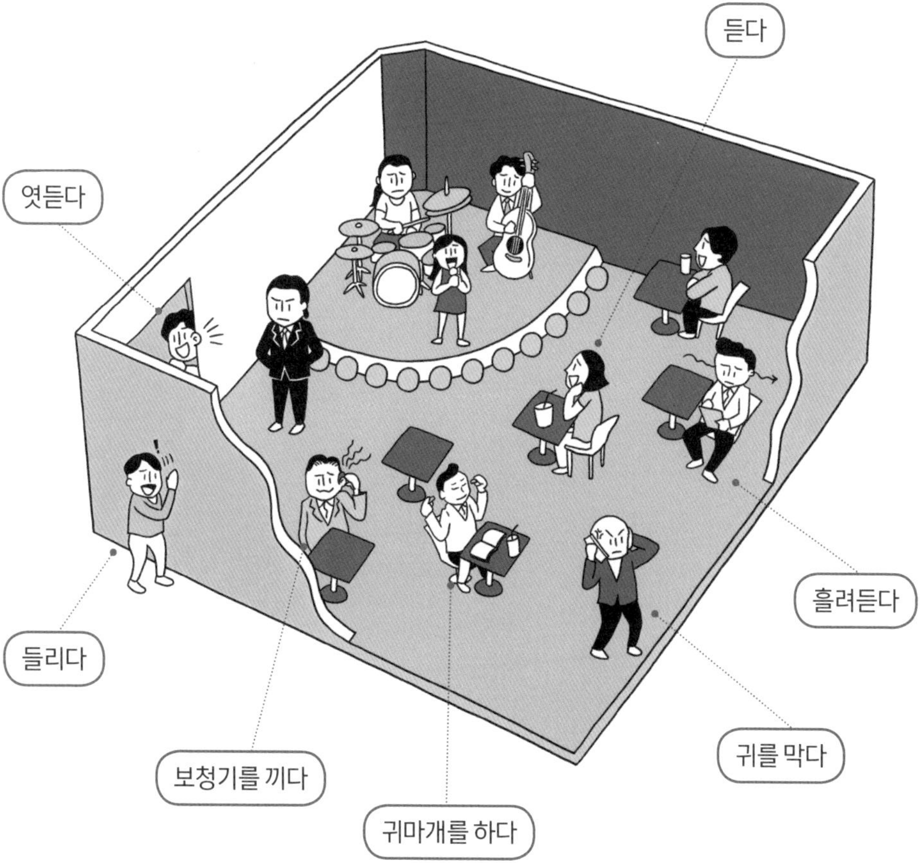

25

듣기

●○

Track #25

엿듣다	to eavesdrop
듣다	to hear, to listen
흘려듣다	to not listen carefully
귀를 막다	to cover one's ears
귀마개를 하다	to wear earplugs
보청기를 끼다	to wear hearing aids
들리다	to sound, to be heard

25

HEARING

듣기

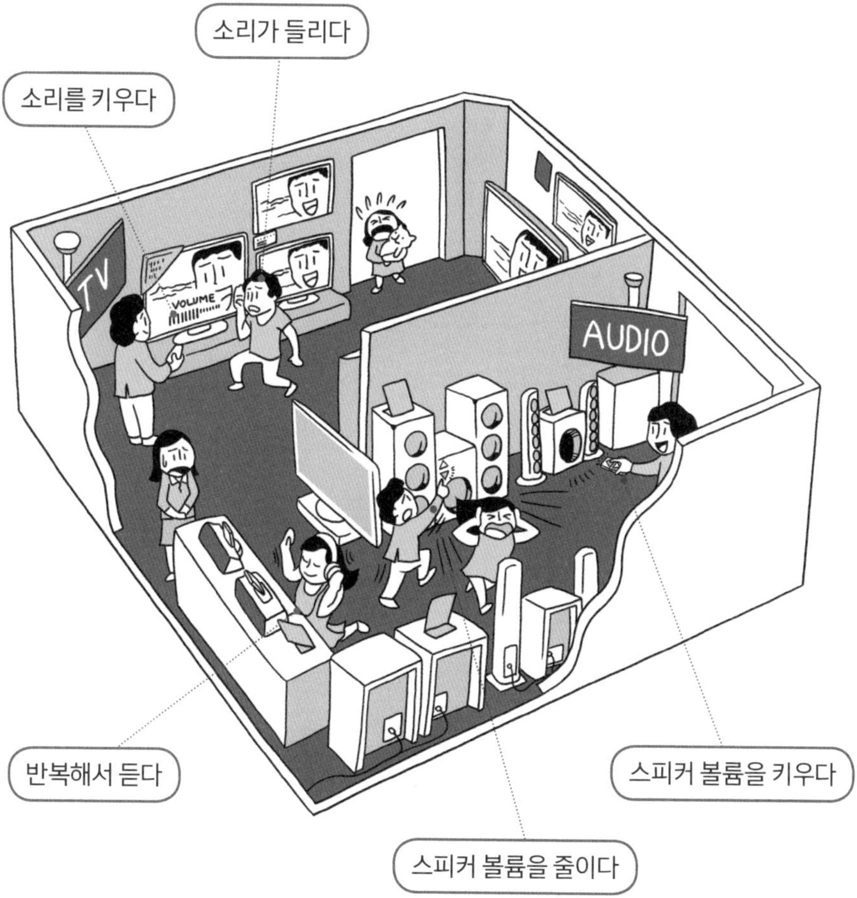

25

듣기

○●

Track #25

소리를 키우다	to turn the volume up
소리가 들리다	a sound is heard
스피커 볼륨을 키우다	to turn the speakers up
스피커 볼륨을 줄이다	to turn the speakers down
반복해서 듣다	to hear/listen repeatedly

26

SEEING

보기

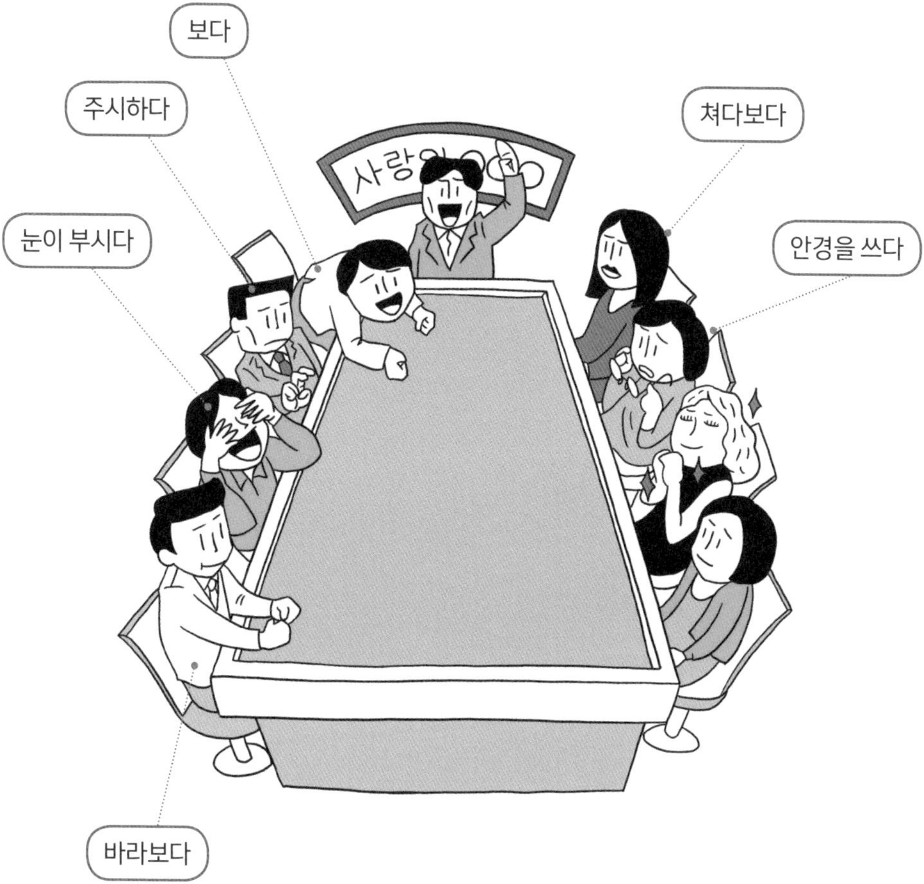

보다
주시하다
눈이 부시다
쳐다보다
안경을 쓰다
바라보다
사랑의

26

보기

●○

Track #26

눈이 부시다	to be dazzling, to dazzle one's eyes; to be blinding
주시하다	to keep an eye on, to watch [someone/something] carefully
보다	to see; to watch
쳐다보다	to look at, to stare
안경을 쓰다	to wear glasses
바라보다	to look at, to stare

*쳐다보다 is sometimes used in a negative way, whereas 바라보다 has a nuance of staring at someone or something with a good feeling.

26

SEEING

보기

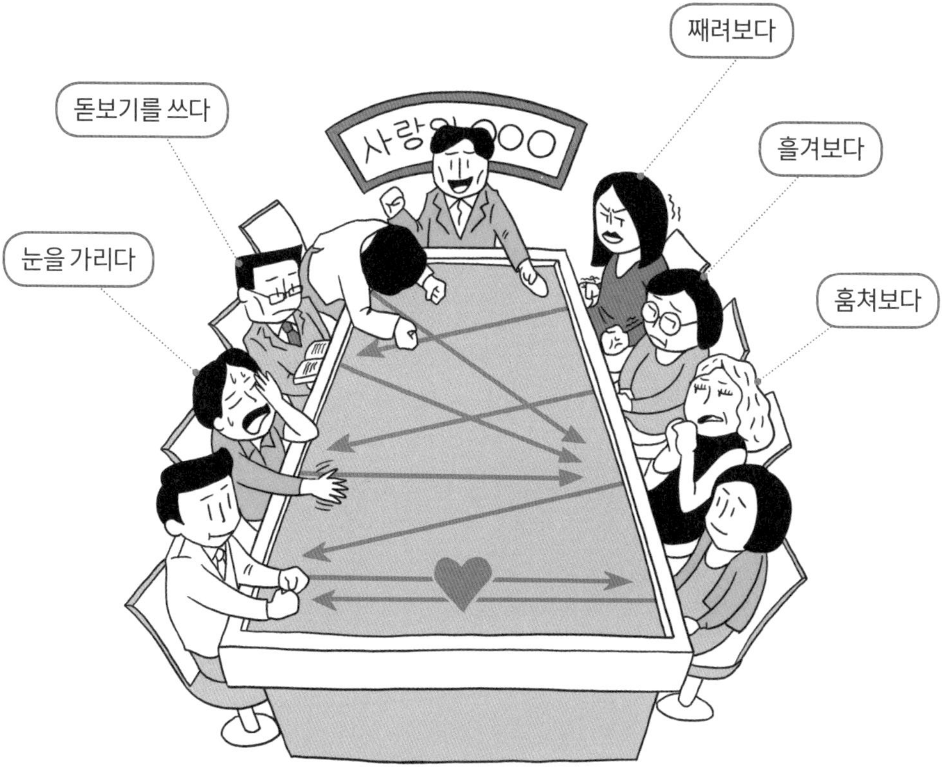

짜려보다
돋보기를 쓰다
흘겨보다
훔쳐보다
눈을 가리다
사랑의 OOO

26

보기

○●

Track #26

눈을 가리다	to cover one's eyes
돋보기를 쓰다	to wear reading glasses
째려보다	to glare
흘겨보다	to give someone a dirty look
훔쳐보다	to sneak a look at

27

TASTING

맛보기

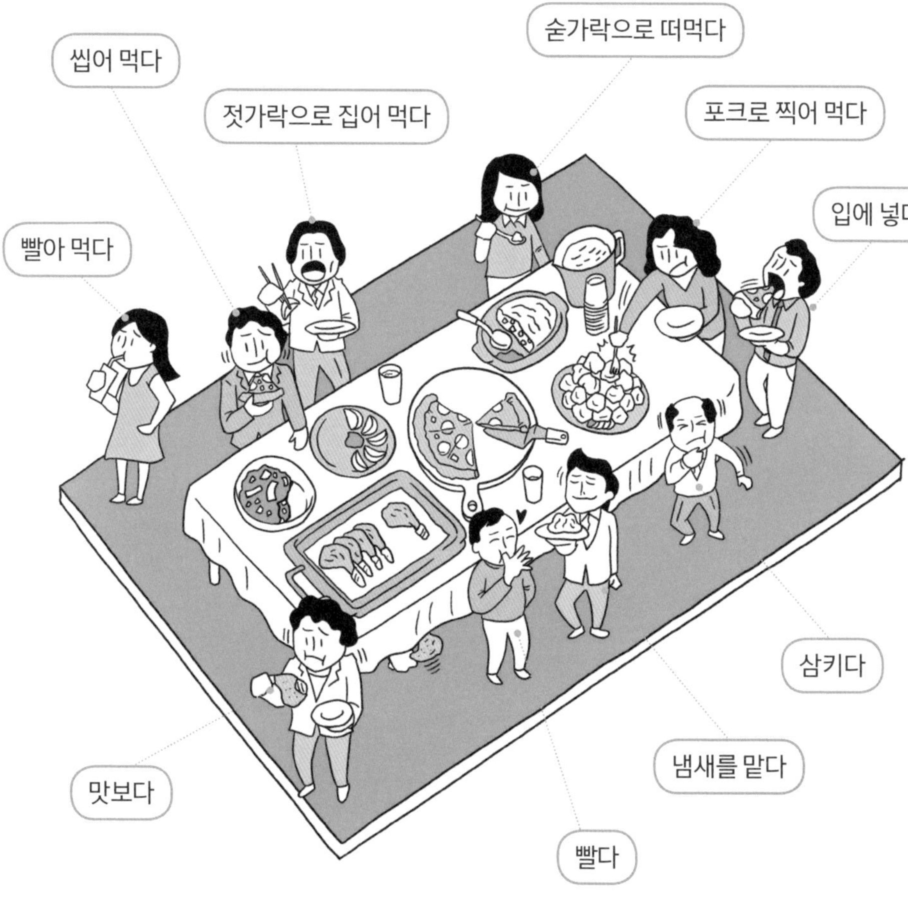

27

맛보기

Track #27

빨아 먹다	to eat by sucking
씹어 먹다	to eat by chewing
젓가락으로 집어 먹다	to pick up and eat with chopsticks
숟가락으로 떠먹다	to scoop and eat with a spoon
포크로 찍어 먹다	to spear and eat with a fork
입에 넣다	to put into one's mouth
삼키다	to swallow
냄새를 맡다	to smell
빨다	to suck
맛보다	to taste

28

TOUCHING

만지기

Track #28

건드리다	to touch; to nudge
만지다	to touch
닿다	to reach; to brush; to touch
쓰다듬다	to stroke, to pet
어루만지다	to pet; to soothe/comfort
주무르다	to rub down, to massage/knead

28

TOUCHING

만지기

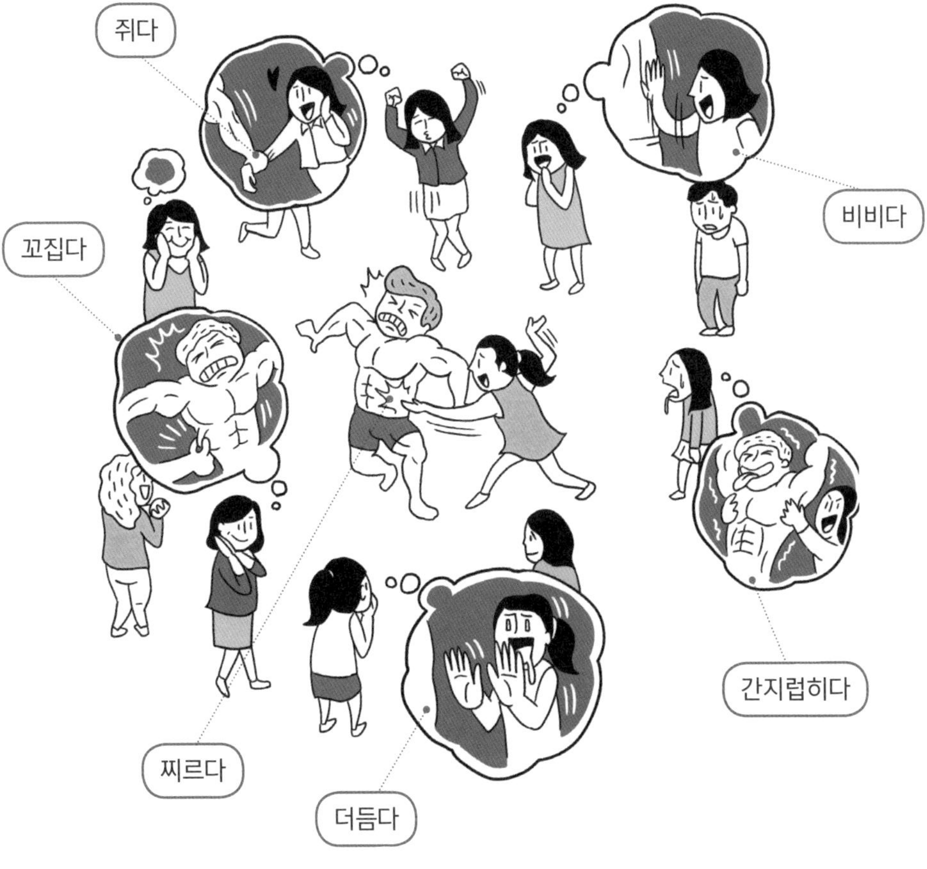

28

만지기

○●

Track #28

꼬집다	to pinch
쥐다	to hold, to grasp
비비다	to rub; to mix
간지럽히다	to tickle
더듬다	to feel; to fumble
찌르다	to poke

29

WALKING

걷기

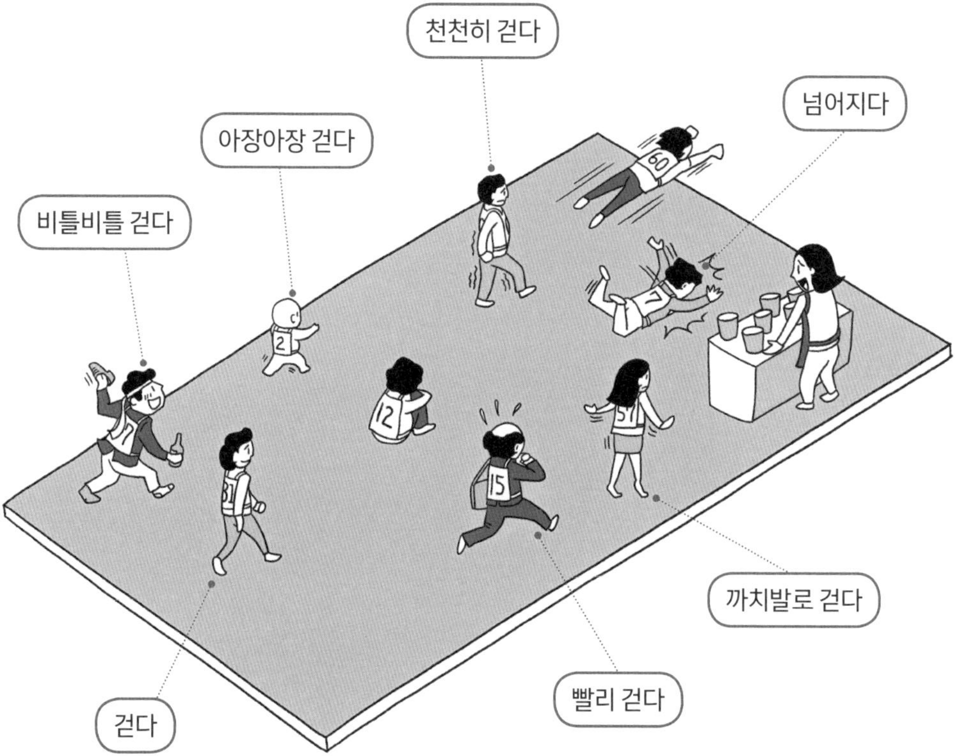

29

걷기

●○

Track #29

비틀비틀 걷다	to stagger; to stumble
아장아장 걷다	to waddle
천천히 걷다	to walk slowly
넘어지다	to fall down
까치발로 걷다	to tiptoe
빨리 걷다	to walk fast
걷다	to walk

29

WALKING

걷기

29

걷기

○●

Track #29

발이 꼬이다	to trip over one's own feet
발을 헛디디다	to lose one's footing; to misstep
다리에 힘이 풀리다	to have no more strength in one's legs
걸려 넘어지다	to trip over something
발을 끌다	to drag one's feet

30

MARRIAGE

결혼

30

결혼

●○

Track #30

축하하다	to congratulate
결혼을 하다	to get married
결혼식을 올리다	to have a wedding ceremony
축의금을 받다	to receive congratulatory money
축의금을 내다	to pay congratulatory money

(30)

MARRIAGE

결혼

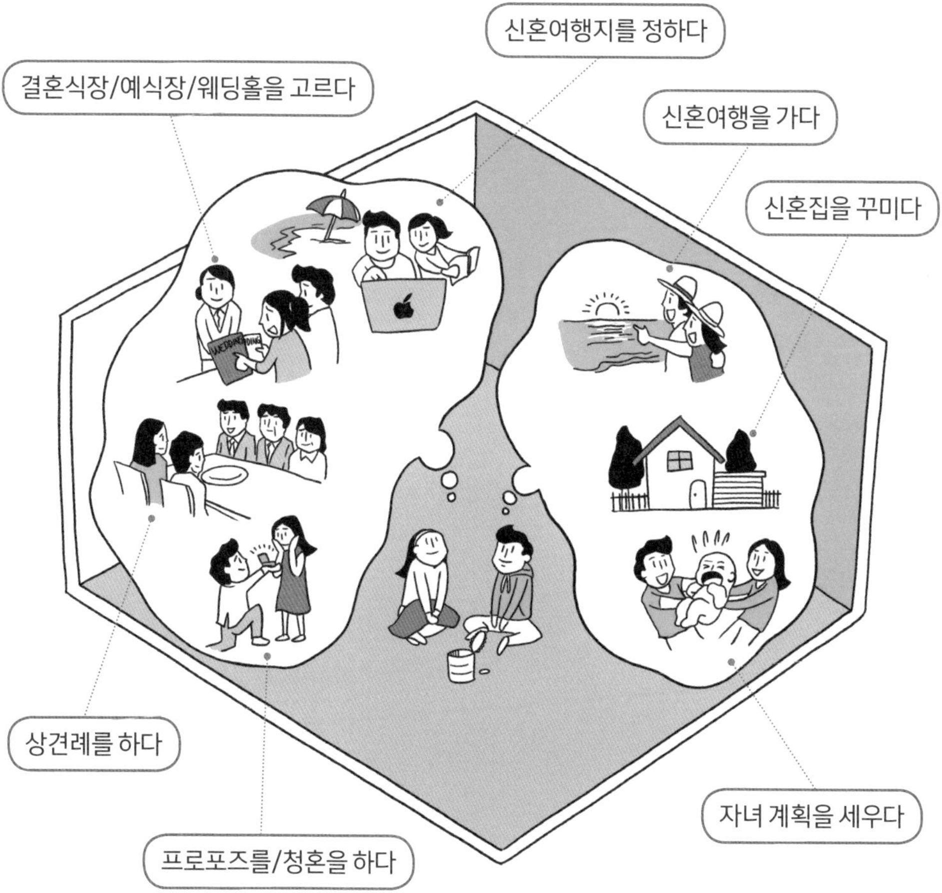

Track #30

프로포즈를/청혼을 하다	to propose
상견례를 하다	to have a meeting between the families of the bride-to-be and the groom-to-be
결혼식장/예식장/웨딩홀을 고르다	to select a wedding hall
신혼여행지를 정하다	to decide where to go for a honeymoon
신혼여행을 가다	to go on a honeymoon
신혼집을 꾸미다	to decorate one's marital home
자녀 계획을 세우다	to plan for having children

BIRTHDAY

생일

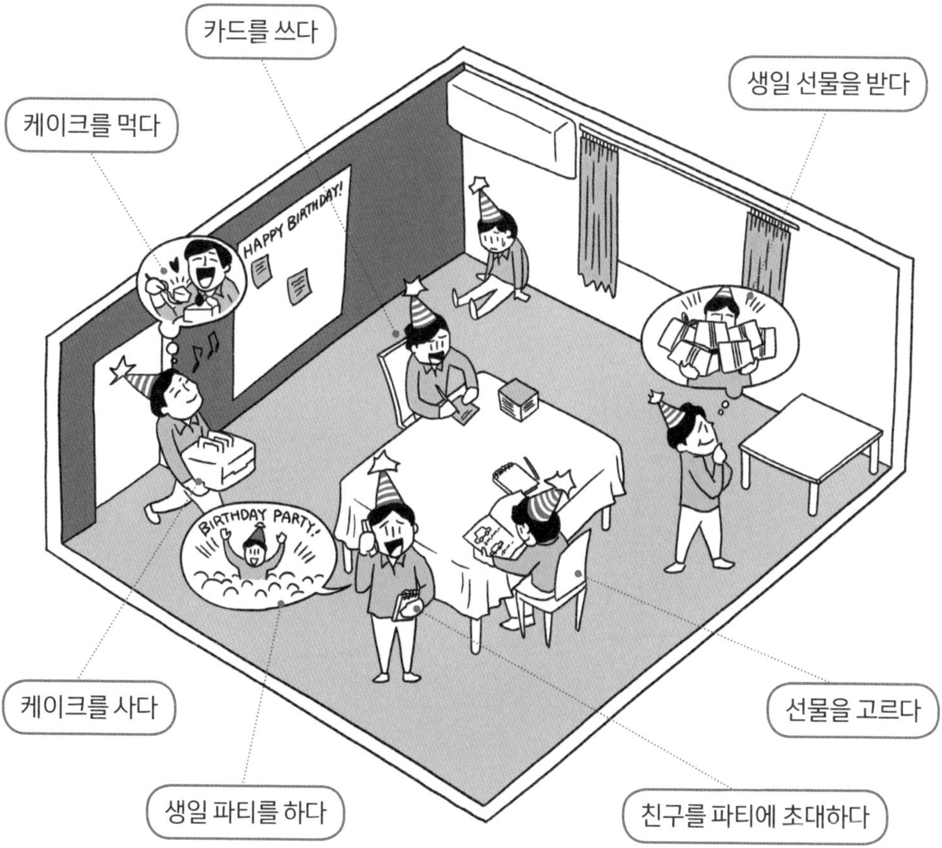
카드를 쓰다
케이크를 먹다
생일 선물을 받다
HAPPY BIRTHDAY!
BIRTHDAY PARTY!
케이크를 사다
선물을 고르다
생일 파티를 하다
친구를 파티에 초대하다

31

생일

●○

Track #31

케이크를 사다	to buy a cake
케이크를 먹다	to eat cake
카드를 쓰다	to write a card
생일 선물을 받다	to get birthday gifts
선물을 고르다	to choose a present/gift
친구를 파티에 초대하다	to invite a friend to a party
생일 파티를 하다	to have a birthday party

31

BIRTHDAY

생일

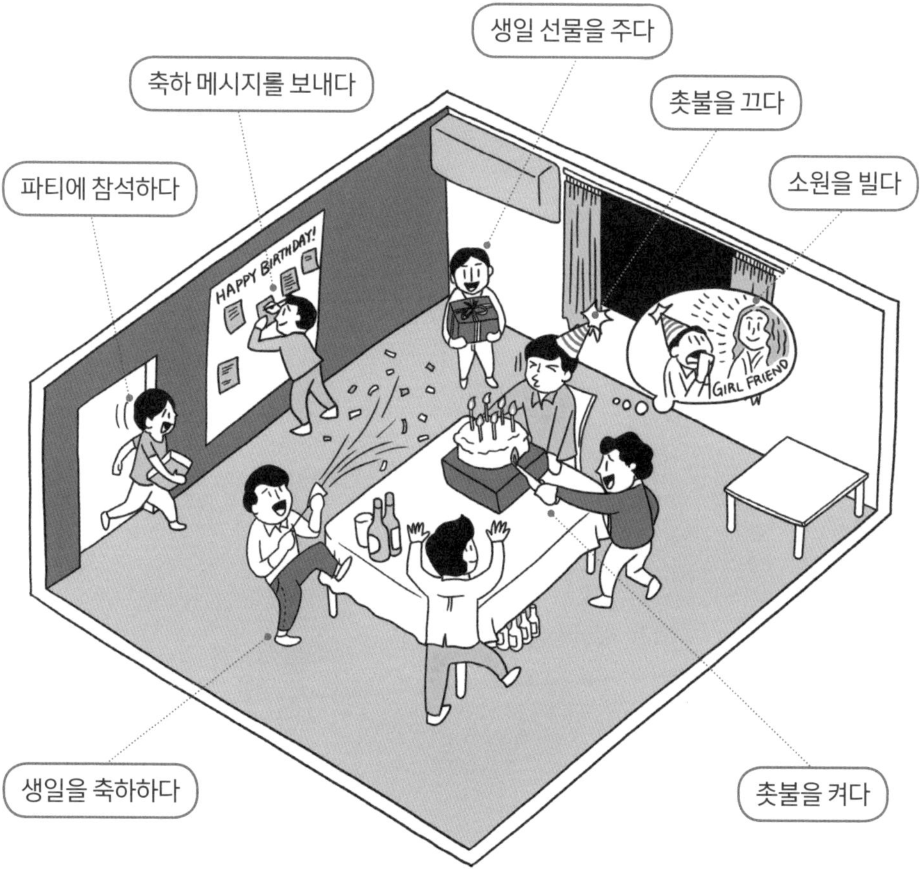

31

생일

∘•

Track #31

파티에 참석하다	to join the party
축하 메시지를 보내다	to send a congratulatory message
생일 선물을 주다	to give a birthday gift
촛불을 끄다	to blow out a candle
소원을 빌다	to make a wish
촛불을 켜다	to light a candle
생일을 축하하다	to congratulate one's birthday

MOVING

이사하기

이사 날짜를 정하다
짐을 옮기다
짐을 싸다
이삿짐 센터를 부르다
도와주다
SEPTEMBER
냉장고를 비우다
이사 나가다

32

이사하기

●○

Track #32

이삿짐 센터를 부르다	to hire a moving company
짐을 옮기다	to move one's stuff
이사 날짜를 정하다	to set a date for a moving
짐을 싸다	to pack
도와주다	to help
이사 나가다	to move out
냉장고를 비우다	to empty out a refrigerator

32

MOVING

이사하기

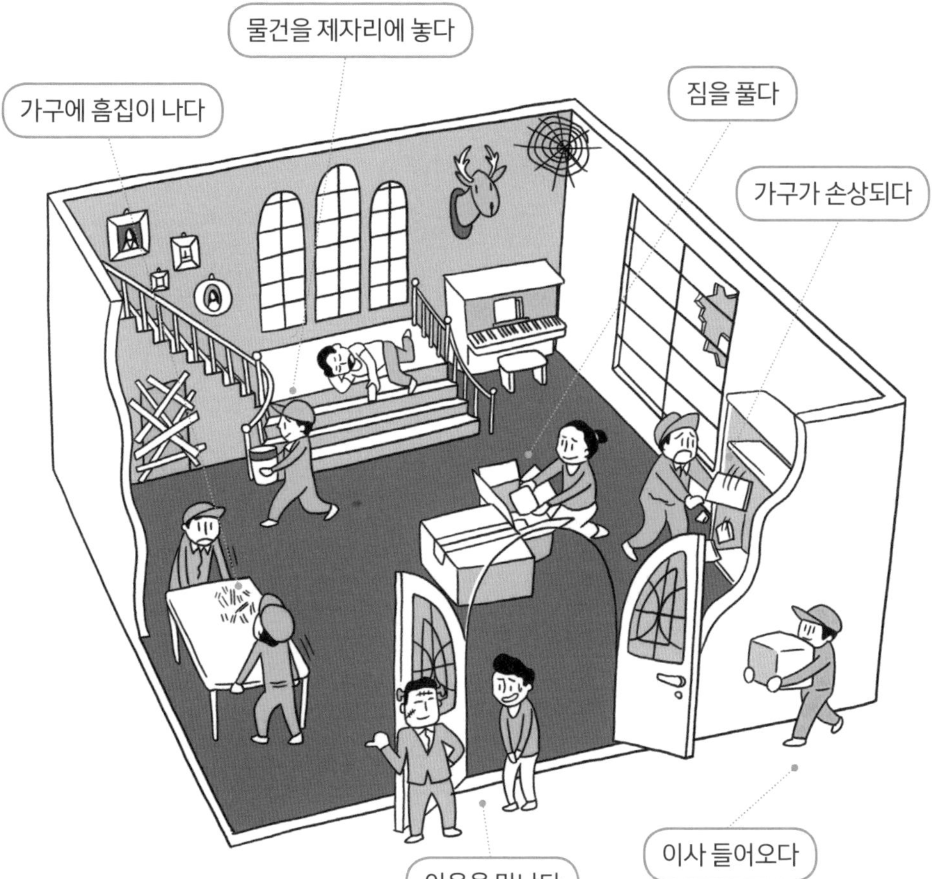

32

이사하기

∘•

Track #32

가구에 흠집이 나다	furniture gets scratched
물건을 제자리에 놓다	to put items back in their place
짐을 풀다	to unpack
가구가 손상되다	furniture gets damaged
이사 들어오다	to move in
이웃을 만나다	to meet neighbors

INDEX

My Daily Routine in Korean

1판 1쇄	1st edition published	2016. 3. 2
1판 3쇄	3rd edition published	2017. 2. 15
지은이	Written by	TalkToMeInKorean
책임편집	Edited by	선경화 Kyung-hwa Sun, 스테파니 베이츠 Stephanie Bates, 김보경 Florence Kim
디자인	Design by	이혜령 Hyeryung Lee
삽화	Illustration by	김수민 Soo Min Kim
녹음	Voice Recording by	선현우 Hyunwoo Sun, 최경은 Kyeong-eun Choi
펴낸곳	Published by	롱테일북스 Longtail Books
펴낸이	Publisher	이수영 Su Young Lee
주소	Address	04043 서울 마포구 양화로 12길 16-9(서교동) 북앤드빌딩 3층
		3rd Floor Book-And Bldg. 16-9 Yanghwa-ro 12-gil, Mapo-gu, Seoul, 04043, KOREA
전화	Telephone	+82-2-3144-2708
팩스	Fax	+82-2-3144-2597
이메일	E-mail	TTMIK@longtailbooks.co.kr
ISBN	979-11-86701-11-9	13710

이 도서의 국립중앙도서관 출판예정도서목록(CIP)은 서지정보유통지원시스템 홈페이지(http://seoji.nl.go.kr)와 국가자료공동목록시스템(http://www.nl.go.kr/kolisnet)에서 이용하실 수 있습니다.(CIP제어번호: CIP2016003599)